JOHN STUD

A
TALENT
FOR
GIVING

Creating a more generous society
that benefits everyone

BLOOMSBURY BUSINESS
LONDON · OXFORD · NEW YORK · NEW DELHI · SYDNEY

BLOOMSBURY BUSINESS
Bloomsbury Publishing Plc
50 Bedford Square, London, WC1B 3DP, UK
Bloomsbury Publishing Ireland Limited,
29 Earlsfort Terrace, Dublin 2, D02 AY28, Ireland

BLOOMSBURY, BLOOMSBURY BUSINESS and the Diana logo are
trademarks of Bloomsbury Publishing Plc

First published in Great Britain 2025

A catalogue record for this book is available from the British Library

Library of Congress Cataloging-in-Publication data has been applied for

ISBN: HB: 978-1-3994-1879-9; eBook: 978-1-3994-1880-5

2 4 6 8 10 9 7 5 3 1

Typeset by Deanta Global Publishing Services, Chennai, India
Printed and bound in Great Britain by Clays Ltd, Elcograf S.p.A.

MIX
Paper | Supporting
responsible forestry
FSC® C018072

To find out more about our authors and books visit www.bloomsbury.com and
sign up for our newsletters

For product safety related questions contact productsafety@bloomsbury.com

'The word "philanthropy" can be loosely translated from Ancient Greek to "love of humanity" – a notion that perfectly sums up this warm, timely book. A generous and profoundly insightful examination of what it means to give, Studzinski explores how we can harness our own unique and distinctive talents to improve the lives of others, and the world around us.'

Dr Maria Balshaw CBE, Director, Tate

'John Studzinski's inspiring new book reveals how rewarding entrepreneurial giving is. By taking action to support others, adapting our specialist knowledge and skills, and giving our time, encouragement and inspiration, we can all make a difference and create positive change for a person or community.'

Barbara Broccoli, Producer

'From one of our leading and celebrated philanthropists, a much welcome Guide to Giving that will inspire a new generation of changemakers to devote their time and energies to the service of others.'

Gordon Brown, former Prime Minister of the United Kingdom

'John Studzinski's invaluable *A Talent for Giving* describes the pilgrimage we can all follow to multiply our unique talents, transform ourselves, and promote the common good. A wonderful book that inspires the temerity of charity.'

Mark Carney, Prime Minister of Canada

'*A Talent for Giving* is the handbook kids need today. It's not a boring lecture. It's a simple plan for finding ways to give in your life. It inspired me to create a new fundraiser at our school in California, and I bet it will help you to give, or give more. You could start by giving this book to a friend!'

Aves Finn-Dean, fifth grader

'Saint Paul famously said that "God loves a cheerful giver". I can imagine no more cheerful giver – nor better guide to giving – than John Studzinski, whose splendid book shows us how to find our talents, take them out of hiding, and invest them in making the world a better one. A wonderful breath of hope!'

Katherine E. Fleming, President & CEO of the J. Paul Getty Trust

'This book is full of wisdom and warmth. It will inspire deep reflection and result in precious new insights, as ancient wisdom is shown to be central to meeting the needs of today. Readers will find themselves challenged, moved and ignited into action.'

Julia Gillard, 27th Prime Minister of Australia

'A deeply compelling and personal exploration of the power of generosity, and the responsibility we all share in creating meaning, socially, personally and spiritually. Blending practical guidance and a true sense of "the good", John Studzinski provides a thoughtful and motivating read for anyone seeking to live with greater empathy, humility, and contribution to the world around them.'

Rupert Goold, Artistic Director

'*A Talent for Giving* will make every reader wiser. With beautiful, straightforward and searching language it tells us how everyone can change the world, one step at the time. I love that idea.'

Erling Kagge, explorer and writer

'*A Talent for Giving* presents powerful insights into the urgency of recognizing our talents and activating them for the greater good of society. Studzinski poignantly illustrates how true giving stems from understanding ourselves and cultivating meaningful relationships. Generosity empowers us to make sustainable contributions, and entrepreneurial giving enriches our lives and communities alike.'

Ken Langone, co-founder, The Home Depot

'John Studzinski knows how to be a true and loyal friend. He has an enormous capacity to give of himself. He listens and is present each and every time. This is a book of love and how to love. It teaches us how to aspire – to find our purpose and how to be human.'

Sybil Lau, philanthropist

'This book is destined to be a classic work in the philanthropy arena. In fact, *A Talent for Giving* might become the most important book for those – hopefully many – far-sighted persons of good will wishing to seek expert guidance on how to fully realize their lives by purposeful entrepreneurial giving.'

Heinrich Liechtenstein, Professor, IESE Business School, Spain

'Giving is part of John's core, whether it is sharing advice with world leaders or dishing up dinner in a soup kitchen, his generosity of spirit is genuine. These qualities make this book an inspirational gift to all who aspire to find their own giving path.'

Karen G. Mills, Senior Fellow Harvard Business School; Former Obama Cabinet Member and Head of the U.S. Small Business Administration

'Perhaps our most meaningful experience in life is a sense of oneness with everyone and everything. We are then propelled to share with others the gifts we have received such as our time, energy, talents and money. Such philanthropy expands our spirit and fills both giver and receiver with peace and joy.'

Ng Kok Song, former Group CIO, GIC

'Generosity enriches both giver and receiver, since a nurturing approach in mentorship and relationships can transform lives. In *A Talent for Giving*, Studzinski champions a uniquely personal approach to philanthropy, building sustainable change and community impact through activated talents. True giving begins with a deep understanding of oneself and one's own talents.'

Indra Nooyi, Former CEO, PepsiCo

'John's clear and passionate call to action is for us to contribute to a more generous society that benefits everyone – drawing on whatever resonates most for each of us whether that is time, talent or treasure. John's faith, that shines through so clearly in this book, makes clear that in return we receive the great gift of fulfillment.'

Ruth Porat, President and Chief Investment Officer, Alphabet and Google

'In both business and philanthropy, I see leadership and engagement as a form of stewardship – a chance to give back by building institutions, backing people, and taking responsibility for long-term impact. What John Studzinski captures in *A Talent for Giving* is that giving isn't separate from enterprise; it *is* enterprise. Whether you're building a career, a company, or a life of purpose, the lessons here will resonate. It is a road map to the good life.'

Tom Pritzker, Executive Chairman, Hyatt Hotels Corporation

'In this timely and inspirational book, *A Talent for Giving*, the philanthropist John Studzinski uses his own journey in entrepreneurial giving to prompt us to explore the ways in which we can each contribute. He uses the language of compassion and encouragement and reminds us of the profound importance of human dignity as we work towards building a generous society. It is a book of quiet and persuasive wisdom.'

Rebecca Salter CBE, President, Royal Academy of Arts

'For John Studzinski philanthropy takes not just kindness but creativity, tenacity and an entrepreneurial spirit. In *A Talent for Giving*, with powerful examples and the wisdom gained over a lifetime of charity, he explains how he did it – and how you can too.'

**Mark Thompson, Chairman of CNN and previously CEO of
The New York Times and Director General of the BBC**

'John Studzinski presents his hard-earned wisdom with great thought and care, imparting readers with the skills needed to engage in the difficult, rewarding work of giving with hope and urgency. This book is an essential reminder that the heavy lifting of building a more just and generous world is never over, and, indeed, begins with each of us.'

Darren Walker, President of the Ford Foundation

'In *A Talent for Giving*, John Studzinski offers inspiration and instruction for developing a lifetime habit of giving – not just in the traditional path of donating or volunteering but by cultivating an entrepreneurial spirit for the common good. With this book, Studzinski invites us to join him in making the world a better place.'

Safa Zaki, President of Bowdoin College

'No good thing is worth having unless it is shared'

Nullius boni sine socio iucunda possessio est

Seneca (Rome, 1st century AD)

This book is dedicated to God
for all the gifts and talents
He has bestowed upon me, His humble servant,
including those of my guardian angel.

CONTENTS

Taking your talent for granted is not an option   xiii

1 Giving: It's all about you   1
2 Beyond the selfie   11
3 You have more talent than you know   17
4 Talents, parables and growth   27
5 The Ts of entrepreneurial giving   43
6 Trailblazing   49
7 Common ground, common sense,
   common good   67
8 Trust is key   77
9 The time of your life   89
10 Hunting for buried treasure   101
11 The power of two   113
12 Toughing it out   129
13 The ties that bind   139
14 Tears of gratitude   153
15 The tech tempest   161
16 Taking a trial run   167
17 Building a generous society   175

Acknowledgements   187
Index   189

TAKING YOUR TALENT FOR GRANTED IS NOT AN OPTION ...

Say the word 'talent' and you immediately evoke something that is natural and inborn. You also evoke something that holds huge potential.

Simply possessing a talent is not enough. If you have a talent, it needs to be defined, nurtured and drawn out. A talent is something to be worked at and worked with. It is worth developing, honing and – in the positive sense of the word – exploiting to the full.

If you're going to make the most of your talent, to put it to the best possible use, it will take some effort on your part. Your ambition and imagination will have a crucial role to play. So will the people around you – family, friends, colleagues, teachers and mentors: they will have their own talents, knowledge, skills and experience to bring to your endeavours.

I've called this book *A Talent for Giving* because it focuses on ways to develop your inherent generosity and empathy. It's about tapping into your impulses for making the world a better place. It's about channelling your passions – even your anger – into a sense of vocation, so that you can apply your talents with real purpose and play a part in creating a more generous society. And it's about doing this energetically, responsibly, and with confidence in yourself and other people, working in a spirit of optimism, creativity and innovation.

A Talent for Giving is also about doing things your own way – not to boost your ego or in a spirit of defiance, but because you have committed to getting the best out of your personal blend of talents. It is about striking your own distinctive path, about building firm structures for giving while retaining flexibility and agility.

I want to help you 'make a go of it'. This is why I place such an emphasis on the principles and practice of entrepreneurial giving.

Entrepreneurial giving is about giving in the broadest sense: you could, of course, be giving money, but you could also be giving your time and your skills, lending your knowledge and resources, or providing emotional support, encouragement and – when your talents are really on a roll – inspiration.

If you succeed in exploiting your true talent for giving, you will find that you get something back, and that is a deep sense of satisfaction and fulfilment. As you follow your entrepreneurial path, the chances are that you will continually find new sources of motivation. Time and again you will discover that you have even more to give – and that will be good for everyone.

1

Giving: It's all about you

It's all about you. This is a book about giving, so why does it open with a phrase so often linked to selfish behaviour?

Here's why: if you are really going to give, it's got to be the real you – every part of you – that's doing the giving. Giving with sincerity, passion and purpose, without a 'personal brand' in mind, and above all joyfully.

Giving, in the broadest sense, is an essential part of life. A gift is any act of kindness or generosity that recognizes and respects the dignity of another human being. It can be something very simple – a smile, or a hug or a few words. And it is a process that works both ways. If you are able to give joyfully, you will receive something in return: validation, satisfaction and fulfilment – maybe more than you could have expected. Giving can prove transformative for both the receiver and the giver, but the transformation doesn't have to be dramatic – it isn't only big gestures and spectacular results that matter. Giving is about taking responsibility for making the connections that we all need, but which our society – fragmented in so many ways – isn't always able to supply.

Why should the idea of giving interest you? It could be that you have reached a pivotal stage in your life. Like everyone else, you were born with certain God-given talents. Those talents have been recognized in some way, by the people around you and by yourself, and you've tried to use them well. You've taken the time to gain an understanding of your purpose. You've gone on to serve that purpose by setting yourself goals and achieving at least some of them. Quite reasonably, you are aiming to achieve a balance in your life – between taking care of yourself and trying to find the best ways of making a difference.

You feel you have a responsibility to make a concrete contribution to society, to play a role in making the world a better place. You might be talking about 'giving back', or possibly even about 'activism'. You probably like the idea of building something together with people who feel and think the same way you do. To use an expression that deserves to be heard more often, you care about the *common good*. That means that you want what's good for the people around you. And what's good for the people around you is good for you too.

In your life so far you might well have achieved more than you think. When you've made things happen, you've done it by following your passions and exercising your talents, by gaining the support and co-operation of people around you. If you really want to make giving happen, it's a question of sticking to the same principles and building on them, consistently and purposefully. Every one of us can make a difference, and we can make the most difference by learning to make the best use of what we have to give.

And the learning never stops. Just keep asking yourself the right questions. What are the passions that drive you to want to give? What frustrates you about the way the world works – or doesn't work? What makes you angry about society? Where do you think it might help to disrupt the status quo? How do you turn conscience and compassion into action? What goals will you set yourself in your giving? How do you keep learning about yourself and your giving? What, in the end, do you want your giving to do for you?

Before you even start asking yourself those questions, there is a fundamental point that needs to be made: giving is not just about money. In fact, it doesn't have to be about money at all. We all have more valuable things to give away.

Think of it this way: money is entirely generic, distinguished only by its quantity. By contrast, your talents and your motivations are highly personal, specific to you. There is an art to giving and your instinct, intuition and inspiration can all play a part in guiding your actions.

Money can still have a role to play – it would be naïve to deny its importance – but it is not the be-all and end-all. Money is an essential tool and it certainly helps make the world go round, but it is not the only tool we have. Money is just one part of the ecosystem of giving: there are other elements that fit around it, balance it and work with it to magnify and sustain its impact.

Giving, like financial investment, can produce multiple returns in the form of benefits for society and for you. We often hear the term 'investment portfolio', but I want you to think about your portfolio for giving. The essentials in that portfolio are your passions, your skills, an element of trust and above all your talents. Money can come later. I want to help you build your portfolio for giving and to think of it as a portfolio for change – for the world and for yourself.

The driver for that change lies in your talents and the way you apply them. Talents, if you identify them accurately, nurture them, and use them with intelligence and sensitivity, constitute an astonishing source of power. Giving, in the broadest sense, is about channelling that power for the common good. I've talked about the need for the real you to be doing your giving. There are potentially powerful parts of the real you – in particular some of your talents – that might not yet be fully discovered. If they are not exactly hidden, they still need to be unearthed and encouraged to flourish.

As you work at drawing out your talents it can make all the difference to benefit from someone else's experience, and maybe I can offer some help here. Over the years I've never stopped building and developing my own portfolio for giving. My thoughts on giving, whether you want to take them on a philosophical level or as a practical guide, are informed by what I have learned over time – from my mistakes as well as my successes. I've made sure never to stop learning or gathering insights from other people, whether they are the people doing the giving, or whether they are the people who stand to benefit from the giving.

My personal principles are also very much bound up with my Catholic faith. It is my spiritual anchor. I talked about giving joyfully and, in one of his letters to the Corinthians, St Paul wrote: 'Each of you should give what you have decided in your heart to give, not reluctantly or under compulsion, for God loves a cheerful giver.'

Of course, my religious faith is not necessarily your religious faith – or you might have no religious faith at all. We all need an anchor and we all have different ways of embracing our spirituality – through religion, meditation, through spending time in nature, or through looking at art or listening to music. And that's fine: what works for me doesn't have to work in the same way for you. The priority has to be your fundamental approach to giving as an integral part of your life.

But no matter what your beliefs, Jesus's famous Parable of the Talents (which will become a recurring theme in this book and which I will explore in Chapter 4) is as relevant to you as it was to me when I started thinking about the principles of giving. The parable, which is found in the Gospel of Matthew, has proved its worth across 2,000 years and many millions of people. It is not about religious beliefs and not exclusively about any relationship you might have with God. It is about taking your life and making something of it. The validity of its message is universal: each one of us has a responsibility, even a duty to make good use of the talents we have been granted.

The Parable of the Talents certainly helped me as I put together my thoughts on giving. My aim is not just to project a vision for giving, but to define a framework and provide stimulus for anyone who wants to develop their talent for giving and produce some benefit for the world. My concern is not with activism, but with activating talent. It is up to you, the person reading this, to take the thinking further by identifying your own strengths, formulating your own strategies for giving, and putting them into action in a way that suits your capabilities and your ambitions.

I will do what I can to get you thinking about giving, to provide a frame of reference so that you can nurture your own beliefs and aspirations. It is up to you to determine your criteria, set your objectives and find a modus operandi that works for you and the people around you. It is certainly not for me to draw conclusions on your behalf. Nor am I going to hand you some kind of 'toolkit' for giving. My intention is much more to help you assemble your own, personally customized set of tools. The best way to do this is to draw on your personal portfolio of beliefs, passions and talents. Once again, it's got to be all about you. Only by going through your own processes and striking your own path will you produce the maximum benefit, for the world and for yourself.

As you follow that path, you might find that the going is not always smooth. You might well encounter some obstacles and setbacks. You might find it is taking you longer than you imagined or expected to reach the destinations you have set yourself. Don't let that deter you. As long as you are continuing to move forward and learning along the way, your efforts will be worthwhile.

People often talk about life and our experiences in terms of a journey, but I'd like to take that idea further. Giving is a journey that can become a pilgrimage. For thousands of years, people of all beliefs have been making pilgrimages to places and sites that are considered sacred. On a pilgrimage we make our way towards an end point where we hope to find enlightenment, spiritual inspiration and renewal.

The late Pope Francis spoke in illuminating and motivating terms about pilgrimages and their significance in a message he sent to a group of pilgrims in 2015: 'Pilgrimage is a symbol of life. It makes us imagine that life is about walking ... Please: do not stand still in life! ... It can happen: we have all had falls, mistakes in life; but if you have made a mistake, get up right away and keep walking.' Traditional religious pilgrimages follow routes that might have been trodden by millions of people over centuries, often travelling in a group. On our pilgrimage of giving, each one of us, guided by our talents, defines our own path.

We all like the idea of making the world a better place. It is within our power to do so, even in a modest way. Once we have identified our talents and have set about putting them to good use through giving, the secret lies in striking a realistic balance between our abilities and ambitions and the time and energy available to us. Whatever the circumstances, we must be ready to take wholehearted responsibility for our actions. At the same time, we must never forget that the act of giving, like so much else in life, means more if we retain a sense of proportion. It also helps to retain a sense of humility. For some reason, 'humility' is not the kind of word we use every day. It's a word with great resonance, but all it means is the quality of being humble. That's a word we *do* hear frequently, perhaps so frequently that it is at risk of losing its deeper connotations.

Ambition and humility are not mutually exclusive: we will achieve more if we don't overreach ourselves. Wisdom lies in taking things step by step. As Mother Teresa of Calcutta once, unforgettably, said to me: 'You can only change the world one person at a time.'

The person who can start to change the world is you.

2

Beyond the selfie

How do you set about changing the world? Your first step is to focus on yourself as you are. If you were taking a selfie, this would be a selfie that only you need to see. A selfie that shows you as you look when you're in the room, up close and personal; a selfie with no filters and no manipulation for public scrutiny. It would also be a selfie that stands to reveal a lot about the person behind the face.

Not that you should consider your selfie as an isolated phenomenon. As you look at it, you should think about yourself in different contexts and how you respond to different people, situations, challenges and opportunities. As you do this, it is of fundamental importance to recognize your talents and strengths. At the same time it makes sense to acknowledge and accept your current limitations. No matter what your aspirations, you need to stay true to yourself.

We live in a competitive world that has been made more competitive by social media and the way it can distort our perceptions. It makes us all too worried about what other people – whether we know them or not – think of us and what we do. It can even make us lose sight of who we really are. Nobody's perfect, no matter how wonderful they make themselves and their lives look. You're not perfect either – and why should you be? Imperfections are part of being human and don't stop us from still having a lot to give. Come to think of it, it is the imperfections we see in other people and the state of the world that can motivate us into giving.

In the greater scheme of things, what matters is what you genuinely have to offer and how you live up to your own ideals. This is not about measuring up to an idealized projected image. By accepting who you really are, and by taking time to understand just how much you have to offer, you make a firm foundation for yourself. You owe it to yourself to be realistic about your shortcomings (we all have them!), but danger lies in defining yourself in terms of what you are *not* – or perhaps in terms of what you are not *yet*. Giving is about sharing, and you can't share what you don't already have. When St Paul – who acknowledged that nobody is perfect by saying, 'None is righteous, no, not one' – wrote about giving, he put it this way: 'For if the readiness is there, it is acceptable according to what a person has, not according to what he does not have.'

'Share' has become an overused word, but sharing in its true sense is about generosity, partnership and participation. If you really want to share, it makes all the difference to have a clear and honest picture of who you are, where your talents lie and exactly what contribution you can make. Remember too that when you share something with other people – just think about sharing a meal – you also get something out of it. If you participate in a successful project for the common good, you share in its benefits. Among those benefits are the relationships you will establish with your partners in the project. These evolve as you gain a deeper understanding of the way your different sets of attitudes and skills can complement and empower each other. Sharing is also about understanding your place in the bigger picture and about encouraging co-operation and continuity.

That bigger picture could be summed up as 'philanthropy', a word that crops up regularly in the media, but not so often in everyday conversation. It literally means 'love of mankind', so the picture it paints is very big indeed. Too big, perhaps, when you are thinking about changing the world one person at a time. In fact, the entire high-level concept of philanthropy is maybe too abstract for the world most of us live in. Maybe it is also too inert, lacking a firm, compelling call to action.

The word 'philanthropy' also carries some daunting baggage. It conjures up images of vast fortunes accumulated over decades or even centuries, powerful dynasties, monumental buildings, gold plaques and massive 'industrial-scale' campaigns with a mission to eradicate disease or hunger. Philanthropic action can seem alienatingly distant from grass roots and 'people like us' – and very much about money rather than anything else we might have to give. For all that, philanthropy – and the philanthropic mindset that drives it – is a force for good: it has achieved wonders in the past and philanthropists today continue to transform thousands or even millions of lives.

In your daily life you probably think more about *charity* than philanthropy. The vocabulary can be tricky here, but my belief is that the two are not synonymous. The word 'charity', like the word 'philanthropy', has its linguistic roots in love, but, for me, it means something different. Charity, as I understand it, is about relieving immediate pain, applying an urgent 'sticking plaster' to a wound. It can be effective, even powerful in the short term, and there will always be a place for charities and charitable action.

Philanthropy, meanwhile, is about achieving permanent change, creating infrastructure and reinforcing solutions that can be sustained in the longer term. There is a huge difference between giving a man a fish – so that he won't go hungry today – and teaching him *how* to fish – so that he won't go hungry tomorrow or the day after that. You might think about donating money to help build a new hospital or school or concert venue, but true philanthropy goes further. It locks into the human capital that must be invested in the future life of that building and its mission to serve society.

My focus is on inspiring ways to produce long-term, sustainable benefits. Even if they turn out to be comparatively small-scale, those benefits are valuable. Remember, you can only change the world one person at a time. That is one of the reasons I will avoid the word 'philanthropy' from now on. It has its place, but is too big and too heavy for this book, too loaded with conventions, implications and assumptions. The word 'giving' is much closer to all of our hearts and lives – and, beyond a positive and generous mindset, it implies positive, concrete action.

We all have it in us to become a 'philanthropist', but what interests me is the part that each of us can play in creating a new vision for giving. Each one of us needs to take this personally and to concentrate on what we can achieve within our own capacities and frame of reference. We're talking about our starting point – that honest, unfiltered selfie – again. Giving is not about what other people think of us, but about what we can do for the world, step by step. We can best achieve our aspirations by taking a realistic approach to building structures and networks that accommodate and amplify our talents.

We shouldn't be afraid of doing things our way, but we need to be honest and realistic about what 'our way' is. It must be a reflection of our true self. Each of us is different and each of us has something distinctive to contribute. We shouldn't tangle ourselves up by worrying what other people think, though we should make room for the opinions of people we really know and trust. By freeing ourselves from received wisdom, we can take a new and enlightened approach to giving, an entrepreneurial approach that recognizes and unleashes the power of our talents to the full.

3

You have more talent than you know

Talent is at the heart of giving, and I mean talent in the broadest sense. It is down to each of us to identify and exercise our particular, personal talents. You could even say that this is part of our duty as members of the human race.

Talent is a source of power and each one of us has the potential to make a difference through giving. That potential lies in the portfolio of talents that each one of us possesses. You will be aware of the talents in your portfolio that are obvious to you. In all likelihood, they will be obvious to the people around you too. But you can be sure that buried in the depths of your portfolio are other talents just waiting to be discovered and activated.

Talent, with its potential to drive purposeful and positive change, is, in my eyes, a gift from God. 'As each has received a gift, use it to serve one another, as good stewards of God's varied grace', was how St Peter expressed it. We receive talent along with the breath of life and it unites everybody on this earth. Your talent plays a crucial role in defining you as an individual. At the same time it can define your value as a member of the community you inhabit, and even your status as a representative of what's good about humankind.

Though talent can be found in all of us, it probably remains the least understood of all human attributes and assets. Even if we are not fully aware of the talents at our disposal, we can be sure that God is. Just take a look at Psalm 139:

> O Lord you have searched me and known me!
> You know when I sit down and when I rise up;
> you discern my thoughts from afar.
> …
> For you formed my inward parts;
> you knitted me together in my mother's womb.
> …
> My frame was not hidden from you,
> when I was being made in secret,
> intricately woven in the depths of the earth.

As God's creations, we are all innately talented in some way and we can all put our talents to good use when it comes to making the world a better place. The irony is that it can be dangerously easy to assume otherwise, because talent as a concept tends to be associated with an elite. When we think of talent, the people who come to mind are the highest achievers, 'stars' who have acquired status in such fields as the arts, sport, science, politics or business. The talent shows we watch in the media are big, noisy, exhibitionist and brutally competitive. The winners selfishly want to take all – and sometimes they do.

Talent has come to be understood as something that determines a hierarchy: 'I'm good at this, but you aren't, so that means I am better than you', or 'You're good at this, but I'm not, so that must mean you are better than me.' The deeper and more important truth is that talent is a leveller: there is a place and a use for every talent, even a 'small' talent.

In a successful working relationship or a winning team, one person's talents will complement those of the other stakeholders. But each of those stakeholders must first take time to identify and define their talents, to understand where they belong in the scheme of things. Where do you have the most to contribute? Where does somebody else best fit in the plan? There is so much to gain if everyone is in a position to be generous with their talents. If you give of your talent, you are sharing the benefit of something that no one else in the world possesses in quite the same way.

Sadly, the majority of people fail to recognize their talents to the full. They think a talent needs to be outstanding – like being a natural for maths, languages, music or sport, or being brilliant at selling and negotiation, or a supreme motivator and organizer. These are the kind of talents that will find a way of shining out. But what about the talents that you hardly know you have? As it happens, simply having self-belief or stamina can be deemed a talent, but talent can just as easily be something less assertive. It can be a 'passive virtue' like patience, or knowing how to be a good listener. What it comes down to is that we all work with the same basic deck of cards, but each of us is wired to play our hand differently.

If your talent is not immediately obvious to you or to the people around you, where and how can you find it? What can you do to *unearth* your talent for giving, to dig it out from the depths of your portfolio?

Before you do anything, remind yourself that it is simply not an option to deny that you have any talent. That certainly isn't the deal with God. All the same, you need to be ready to accept that not everyone can play all the aces in life. Wherever you find yourself, there is a valuable role in life and society for people who play twos and threes.

The essence of your talent lies at the intersection of your background, your intuition, your abilities and your values. It is your duty – and your privilege – to develop it, and your first step is to think about the activation points in your life.

Just what are you really good at? What spurs you into confident action and what makes you feel good in your interactions with other people? What are your aspirations for yourself and for the people around you? What are your principles and your passions? And by that I mean your passion for the things you love, but also your passion for putting right what's wrong with the world.

The power of your talent lies in how people respond to you and in how you respond to them – what you have to offer them, what you give to them, and how you make things better for them. Through your talent you will boost their self-esteem and confidence, and that in turn will provide a boost for you. The more comfortable and empowered you feel, the stronger your position when it comes to giving. In essence, the impetus for giving, for contributing to the common good, arises at the point where your own needs meet the needs of society. To borrow a phrase from St Paul, 'Therefore encourage one another and build each other up.' We are talking mutual benefits here.

Successful and fulfilling interaction shines a light on your talent, whether your contact is with other members of a team, with someone in a position of authority, with someone you trust and love, or even with someone you see as a potential or active adversary. Whatever the context, you need to keep your eyes and mind open. Never rule out the possibility that you have further talents to be discovered. Once your light bulb moment has happened, once you have been *activated*, you must be ready to run with your ideas – to explore your talent further and to define how best to put it to good use.

HOW DO YOU UNEARTH AND ACTIVATE YOUR TALENTS?

Start by building on your experience. Take some time to do some thinking …

- Think back to the 'lightbulb' moments in your life – as a child and as an adult. Those moments when you realized you were able to do something you had maybe thought was beyond you.
  - How did you arrive at those moments? What about the times when you had to take on a challenge that you weren't prepared for – and made a success of things?
  - What did you learn about yourself?
  - What did your response tell you? What about the responses of other people?
  - What difference did that realization make to your life and the lives of the people around you?

- Think about the talents you discovered at those moments. How could you apply them today with an eye to the common good? Focus on the past few days.
  - Where did you feel you rose to some kind of challenge – large or small and possibly unexpectedly?
  - What were the talents that you ended up activating?

A talent for action? Your strengths and your weaknesses

- When it comes to making things happen, what are three talents that you think you have?
  - ◦ Now ask some people you trust what they think your three talents are.
  - ◦ How do the results match up? Are there any surprises?
  - ◦ Now go through the same exercise, but this time pinpoint three weaknesses that might compromise your ability to make things happen.
  - ◦ You need to recognize those weaknesses, but don't let them undermine your confidence. Think about ways to compensate for them, or even to overcome them.

Identifying a talent is one thing, but how do you best activate it and develop it into a talent for giving?

As I said, the impetus for giving arises at the point where your own needs meet the needs of society. Take a look at your immediate environment or your community, or at society more broadly. What are the issues that trigger your passions – your anger, your compassion and your sense of justice as much as your enthusiasm? My belief is that the most powerful way to engage with those issues – and to make the biggest difference for the people involved – is to take an entrepreneurial approach to giving, an approach that grows from your talents and which is shaped by you.

Even if your talents are doing the driving, you are likely to need someone on hand who can build your confidence and know-how. There is always something to be learned. It makes all the difference to receive mentoring and encouragement, from your peers and from people with greater or different experience. Sometimes that mentoring and encouragement is offered to you spontaneously. At other times you might have to search it out. In the same way, we all need structures and communities that can accommodate our talent and support it as we put it into action.

TAKING YOUR TALENT FURTHER

- In your personal or professional sphere, are there people you admire for the contribution they make to your community or to society more broadly?

Once you've identified your talent and are ready to develop it, why not approach these people for some advice on applying your talent to giving? If you know groups or organizations that you feel are making a difference to the world, go and talk to them. Find out if you can become a resource for them, even on a trial basis – and whether in the process they can help develop your talent for giving.

Entrepreneurial giving is about going your own way, but with a focus on developing your talents and applying them for the sake of the common good. In any situation where you're taking an entrepreneurial approach – taking the initiative, trying something new and putting your thoughts into action – you should be prepared for some frustrations and some (hopefully constructive) criticism. If you see everything as an opportunity to learn, you will build on your strengths and expand your horizons. In the end, entrepreneurial giving stands to validate your talent and your worth as a member of society, providing you with satisfaction and reassurance. But there is always more to be done and more that you can do. Nurture your portfolio of talent, believe in it, invest it wisely and it will keep growing.

4

Talents, parables and growth

Parables are not just something you'll find in the Bible. They are meant for you, as you live now. Above all, they help you understand yourself. You might have first heard about the Parable of the Talents at school. Your impression might be that it's just an old story, and it is – found in the Gospel of Matthew – but you might be surprised by the straight-talking tone it takes. It might surprise you even more to discover how directly it applies to your life today.

Two thousand years on from the time of Jesus, it serves us as a source of wisdom – what we might now call an exercise in thought leadership. The parables that Jesus told, and which are reported in the Gospels, provide vivid and memorable analogies for the everyday situations and challenges we still face. They form a bridge between Biblical times and our existence in the twenty-first century. It is up to each of us to consider the example presented by the Parable of the Talents, to recognize its implications and to apply its thinking in our own life. If there are universal truths in the Bible, they are universal because they are relevant to each and every one of us.

Among the most famous parables are the stories of The Prodigal Son – which offers us a lesson in humanity and generosity – The Lost Sheep, The Sower and the Seed and, last but definitely not least, the Parable of the Talents. The parables are designed to grab our attention. They often make their points in graphic, dramatic terms. Taken at face value, they can sometimes even seem harsh, aiming to catch us out and pull us up. In highlighting the challenges we face and the mistakes we might make, they speak to our vulnerability. If we acknowledge those challenges and make up our minds to tackle them, the parables equip us to navigate our lives with greater confidence.

God is a good father. He guarantees us his unconditional love, but he also leaves us space to exercise our free will. He understands that we will generally do our best to get things right as we make the effort to unearth, nurture and share our talents. Developing our relationship with our talents will take some thought and care, and the parables can help keep us on the right track. If we are really going to try and make the world a better place, we have to devote time and energy to building trust – trust in ourselves and trust in other people.

But God, giving us the freedom to make mistakes, also gives us the opportunity to learn. We all make errors of judgement or simply get things wrong. After all, we are only human. We can only start to get things right again if we recognize how, where and why we made our mistakes. If we want to do better, we have to take responsibility for our decisions and actions and for our talents. The parables, with their striking images, strong messages and multiple perspectives, can serve to point us in the right direction. You can take yourself further by accentuating the positive – by consciously unearthing your talents and cultivating them in ways that benefit you, the people close to you and the broader community.

The value of talent – if you activate and nurture it to release its full potential – can be enormous. We will often be quick to recognize real talent in someone else. But strangely, we can be slow to realize the full truth of our own talents.

At the time Jesus was alive, what was known as a talent was immediately recognizable. It was wholly tangible and highly valuable. Unlike talent as we know it today, it was also hard, cold and impersonal. Taking its name from the Greek *talanton*, a talent was a unit of weight and money. It was valuable – equivalent to up to 20 years' worth of a labourer's wages at a time when, on average, a man could expect to live maybe 35 years. This talent, this substantial unit of currency, is what Jesus uses as a metaphor in his parable. It is a parable that remains powerfully relevant to talent as we understand it in our own time.

Here is talent as it appears in the Gospel of Matthew, Chapter 25. When Jesus talks about the 'kingdom of heaven' here he doesn't mean 'somewhere up in the clouds with pearly gates'. What he is talking about is God's presence on earth, expressed through us and our lives. When God touches us and blesses us with talents, he makes us human. The kingdom of heaven lies in the way we bring our talents and our values into play as we interact with other human beings and how we invest ourselves in the cause of the common good.

For the kingdom of heaven is like a man travelling to a far country, who called his own servants and delivered his goods to them. And to one he gave five talents, to another two, and to another one, to each according to his own ability; and immediately he went on a journey. Then he who had received the five talents went and traded with them, and made another five talents. And likewise he who had received two gained two more also. But he who had received one went and dug in the ground, and hid his lord's money. After a long time the lord of those servants came and settled accounts with them.

So he who had received five talents came and brought five other talents, saying, 'Lord, you delivered to me five talents; look, I have gained five more talents besides them.' His lord said to him, 'Well done, good and faithful servant; you were faithful over a few things, I will make you ruler over many things. Enter into the joy of your lord.' He also who had received two talents came and said, 'Lord, you delivered to me two talents; look, I have gained two more talents besides them.' His lord said to him, 'Well done, good and faithful servant; you have been faithful over a few things, I will make you ruler over many things. Enter into the joy of your lord.' Then he who had received the one talent came and said, 'Lord, I knew you to be a hard man, reaping where you have not sown, and gathering where you have not scattered seed. And I was afraid, and went and hid your talent in the ground. Look, there you have what is yours.' But his lord answered and said to him, 'You wicked and lazy servant, you knew that I reap where I have not sown, and gather where I have not scattered seed. So you ought to have deposited my money with the bankers, and at my coming I would have received back my own with interest. So take the talent from him, and give it to him who has ten talents.'

For to everyone who has, more will be given, and he will have abundance; but from him who does not have, even what he has will be taken away.

The Parable of the Talents does not make comfortable reading for any of us. It is an exercise in tough love, highlighting the risks if we fail to recognize the true nature of our gifts. At the same time it gives us some hope, suggesting that any benefits we achieve will be multiplied if we genuinely put our gifts to good use. It gets us thinking about what we can make of our gift of talents if we activate them and invest them for the common good.

When you read and re-read this parable, with an open mind and an open heart, you will recognize yourself in it. It is up to you to draw the conclusions that are relevant to you and the way you think and behave. Which of the three servants is most like you? Are you a natural entrepreneur like the five-talent man – a bit of a risk-taker, perhaps? Or, in the vein of the one-talent man, do you err too heavily on the side of caution? Or perhaps, like the two-talent man, you tend to strike a reasonable balance, but maybe could do better.

The truth is that each of us can be any one of those three servants. No one manages to be five-talent man in every aspect of their life. Our performance depends on the situation we find ourselves in at a particular moment or at a specific stage in our evolution. An investor stewards a portfolio of investments, and on the same principle, each of us stewards our portfolio of talents. And, like an investment, a talent can underperform if it is poorly managed or simply gets forgotten – buried like the third servant's talent. On the same theme, your portfolio of talents, like an investment portfolio, will benefit from being well balanced and from being 'worked' to produce the best yield possible. Not every investment will yield a dramatic profit, but at the least you should look for a decent return on each of your talents.

Unlike investments, you can't delegate your portfolio of talents to a specialist professional. It is up to you to take the active role in managing your portfolio, to build on your strengths of course, but also to identify your weaknesses. Above all, through unearthing and nurturing your talents, you will develop and balance your portfolio.

When it comes to working with other people, whether as a pair or as part of a larger team, you are once again dealing with a portfolio of valuable and complementary talents. The members of a successful team do not necessarily excel in the same areas of endeavour. They need to acknowledge this by taking responsibility for understanding their talents and applying them consciously and cannily, but also in a spirit of generosity.

Let's take a look at the parable in terms of talent as we understand it today. We can infer from it that the talents we are blessed with – whatever they are – should be unearthed, developed and put to use in a way that produces a return.

Like the third servant, we might already be guilty of squandering our talent – in danger of losing something we possess – simply by not bringing it to light. The parable's final paragraph reminds us of the need to nurture our talents and apply them well, to our benefit and to the benefit of the people around us; in other words to the common good. Otherwise we will stagnate. We might even risk losing the talents we are lucky enough to have been given in the first place.

And what about the servants' 'lord', their boss? In the parable, he is a proxy for God (acting in tough, Old Testament form). How about we take him at face value, not as a metaphor but as another human being? For instance, should he show some compassion and greater generosity of spirit? After all, he has a responsibility and duty of care to those three people who are in his service. Yes, he rewards the two servants who invest successfully by making each of them 'ruler over many things', but he acts angrily and harshly towards the third servant, who is already in a vulnerable position. He is striking a man when he is down.

The boss is clearly a man who has talents in the modern sense. For a start, he is successful in material terms. He is also an astute judge of his staff's abilities, as he demonstrates in the way he allocates the money in line with each servant's potential. But that doesn't mean he has nothing to learn about nurturing talent. His approach to the third, over-cautious servant is to instil fear. Doesn't he realize that he will end up stifling whatever talent the servant might have to offer? Based on his existing insights, the boss would have done better to devote some time to advising that underperforming servant, to mentoring and *investing* in him. That would have been far more constructive than putting him to a test he was clearly likely to fail. By acting in an intimidating, autocratic way, the boss has ended up wasting time, treasure and talent.

If the boss had taken a different approach by becoming a mentor to his anxious servant, he would have stood to learn something along the way. Mentoring is a reciprocal process, very different from the conventional 'command and obey' relationship between a boss and employee. A more nurturing approach would have benefited the boss in human terms – and possibly in material terms too: after all, in the parable his servants are investing his money, not their own. It is to his advantage if his servants enjoy success in investing their talents.

When you read the Parable of the Talents, you might end up feeling guilty about not making enough of the gifts you possess. But feeling guilty won't do you – or anybody else – any good. It is far better to take responsibility, to draw a positive message from the parable and above all to recognize its call to action: make the most of the talents granted to you. There is nothing to be gained from being afraid to use and develop your talents. This might well involve pushing yourself beyond your comfort zone. You need to be ready to defy the everyday expectations that you're in the habit of setting yourself or which you encounter in your daily interactions, whether face-to-face or on social media.

There will always be an element of risk and uncertainty in life, but you can only evolve and grow if you are ready to experiment. In entrepreneurial mode, you must be ready to learn from your failures as well as your successes. Life is an iterative process, of taking steps forward, but also of taking the occasional step backward. The important thing is to keep moving in the right general direction. There is a great line in St Paul's letter to the Philippians: 'But one thing I do: forgetting what lies behind and straining forward to what lies ahead, I press on toward the goal.'

Fail to keep moving and, like the third servant in the parable, you end up stagnating. Lacking the courage to believe in his own potential, he ignores his single talent by burying it in the ground. His boss, seeing things in black and white and completely from his own standpoint, reprimands him for being wicked and lazy.

Very few of us are wicked, but nearly all of us, at least from time to time, will try and take the easy route. We can fail to make a special effort. We can even become complacent. It is far better for everyone if we can keep challenging ourselves, putting energy into understanding our talents so that we can believe in them and make best use of them. Once we are confident in ourselves, we can take the kind of calculated risks that define an entrepreneurial approach.

The 'wicked and lazy' servant's lack of entrepreneurial spirit is symbolized in the way he buries his talent in the ground. By contrast, you could choose to bury (symbolic) *seeds* in the ground. To favour a strong yield you would choose your spot with care and you'd dig, turn, water and fertilize the soil. You'd care for your plants as they grew. You'd be showing some entrepreneurship. It would take some thought and some work – and there would always be a risk that your crop might fail, or at least not turn out as well as you hoped – but you'd be showing some vision. You'd be putting some effort into maximizing your chances of success, into making your garden grow.

No matter how hard you work at whatever you do, you won't make best use of your time and energy by comparing yourself to other people – which is what social media so often prompts us to do. That's what St Paul thought too. He wrote: 'Not that we dare to classify or compare ourselves with some of those who are commending themselves. But when they measure themselves by one another and compare themselves with one another, they are without understanding.' What really matters is how you live up to your own talents and expectations.

In the parable, the boss compares the performances of the three servants. Each of them, whether judged a success or a failure by their boss, would do well to hold up a mirror to himself – it's that brutally honest selfie moment again. Each of them can gain a closer, sharper understanding of their achievement and potential. Five-talent man might decide to strike a new path for himself as an entrepreneur rather than putting all his efforts into doubling his master's money. Two-talent man should consider upping his competent game. If he is to survive, one-talent man has to find the courage to reinvent himself.

The boss could benefit from some introspection too. He should maybe consider the value that lies in transferring knowledge to his servants – further building their confidence (and his income) and sharpening their professional skills. He could give one-talent man another chance by taking a lead from another parable, in the Gospel of Luke. It tells of a man who is advised not to cut down a fig tree that has failed to produce fruit three years in a row – instead he should give it one more year and one more opportunity. Who knows, by showing some compassion and generosity of spirit, the boss could both get a further yield on his investment and give himself a nice warm glow along the way.

For me, the real moral of the story is that we should never be complacent about our talents – or wary of using them. Instead, we should engage in a constant process of discovery and development. Every talent we have is intrinsically more valuable, even exponentially more valuable, than we could ever realize.

But to grow talent and apply it successfully takes work – trial and error and commitment. You can never just leave your talents to nurture themselves; it is up to you to stimulate and sustain them. Do that and you will keep moving forward and you will keep setting a positive example: you will stand a greater chance of making a happy ending for the parable you tell with your life.

The Parable of the Talents ends with some resonant and challenging words: 'For to everyone who has, more will be given, and he will have abundance; but from him who does not have, even what he has will be taken away.'

Your talents are God-given – and God won't take them away – but it is your job to unearth them. Don't deprive yourself of something that's already within your grasp. Embrace the possibilities offered by your talent and do all you can to turn them into reality. The words of the parable are not as cut-and-dried as they might at first appear – it is up to you to interpret them in your own way, in the light of your own talents and potential. Otherwise, you risk accepting limitations in your life, and limiting your capacity for giving.

Now could be a good moment to take another, fresh look at the Parable of the Talents. Where exactly do you see yourself in it and what would you do next if you were one of the servants?

The last sentence of the parable is bound to stay in your mind. Its messages are echoed in a line from another story of masters and servants in the Gospel of Luke: 'From everyone to whom much is given much will be required, and from the one to whom much is entrusted more will be demanded.' There can be no resting on your laurels, even when you have notched up some successes. The responsibility is always there to do as much as you can with what you have, and to give to the maximum. As Jesus also said: 'It is more blessed to give than to receive.'

To make the most of your giving – for the sake of the people around you and for yourself – you have to start by making the most of what you have. A less widely known parable, the Parable of the Mustard Seed, sheds some light on this. You can find it in the Gospels of Matthew, Mark and Luke and this is how it reads in the first of those:

> The kingdom of heaven is like a mustard seed, which a man took and planted in his field. Though it is the smallest of all seeds, yet when it grows, it is the largest of garden plants and becomes a tree, so that the birds come and perch in its branches.

This makes me think of the saying 'From tiny acorns mighty oaks do grow.' Over a period of time, small projects and small, but consistent successes can mount up to something big.

Start off by unearthing and activating your talents. Apply them to an initiative you believe in – however small – and nurture it with purpose and consistency. Amplify your efforts through motivating and mentoring other people and you can grow your initiative into something robust and sustainable. Do all this and you will enhance, support and enrich the lives of other people. That is surely the essence of giving.

5

The Ts of entrepreneurial giving

'Talent' is a word that has already come up many times in this book, but it is just one of the words beginning with T which encapsulate the principles of entrepreneurial giving.

All the Ts link back to talent in some way: talent is the fundamental T, the consistent touchpoint. Your talent sets all the other Ts in context for you, infusing them, resonating with them and multiplying their effect. It is through the application of your talent that the other Ts become most powerful and productive.

Here, then, is a summary of the Ts of entrepreneurial giving. Keep an eye out for each T as you read this book. Think about the role that each T already plays in your life, and think about the role it could play as you undertake your giving pilgrimage, unearthing and developing your entrepreneurial talents for giving and building your own 'giving enterprise' or 'giving venture'.

- **Talent**

Talents are the building blocks of entrepreneurial giving. We all have talents, but we are not always aware of every talent we have. An entrepreneurial approach to giving starts with identifying and activating the talents we know we have. Beyond that, it entails making an effort to unearth talents that we are not fully aware of having, or which we might be reluctant to acknowledge because we are not sure what to do with them. (Just think of the anxious servant in the Parable of the Talents, who is frozen into inaction.) Once your talents are unearthed and defined, you can channel, or even unleash them through giving.

- **Time**

Time is perhaps the most precious gift we have and the most precious gift we can make. But as precious as it is, we can all be prone to waste it. And no matter how busy we think we are, we are all in a position to give of our time. Time spent giving is time well spent.

- **Treasure**

Treasure might seem to be synonymous with money. But treasure is something more than money. Money becomes treasure when it is donated or used in a context where talent has been activated and trust can be taken as read. Treasure, as we all know, is sometimes buried. It takes talent to unearth it. Perhaps you could even say that talent's transformational potential makes it like the legendary Philosopher's Stone of the medieval alchemists (and Harry Potter!): it can turn the base metal of everyday money into golden treasure.

- **Trust**

In your heart and soul you understand trust, but do you fully appreciate the role it can play in giving? Trust is the essential complement to talent, time and treasure. It binds them together and boosts their value. Being able to give your trust to someone is in itself a gift. If you are able to trust in other people – and they are able to trust in you – the potential and power of your giving is multiplied.

- **Temperament**

Temperament is your motivation to take action. Temperament can be the anger you feel when you see injustice or suffering, or when you are faced with threats to the future of humanity or the world. Or temperament can be the passion for change that fuels your entrepreneurial drive.

- **Tenderness**

Tenderness is the complement to temperament. It is more than kindness; it is a deep and enduring sense of compassion. It tempers temperament, transforming anger into a force for good and reminding you where to direct your passions. In your giving, tenderness infuses your relationship with each person or being you aim to help. Tenderness is a 'soft' emotion, but in entrepreneurial giving it coexists with a thread of steely tenacity. I think of Mother Teresa of Calcutta, Diana, Princess of Wales and Cardinal Basil Hume, Archbishop of Westminster, all of whom I often watched as they gave love and compassion. They were tender, but also brave, tenacious and purposeful as they took action or motivated other people to act.

• Temerity • Tenacity • Toughness

As an entrepreneur, you will be ready to challenge the status quo and question conventional thinking. Sometimes, you will have to go against the grain or maybe even defy authority. There will be times when you will need to be brave and take calculated risks. If you are going to make things happen, you will sometimes need to get favours out of people – and you have to be prepared to ask for those favours.

Even so, you won't always achieve your aims as quickly as you would like. People will say 'no' to you, but that shouldn't stop you from trying again when the moment is right. And on occasion, you will be the person who finds a reason to say 'no' when someone asks you for help. The entrepreneurial approach holds challenges, but ultimately you will find that temerity, tenacity and toughness come together in the form of resilience – the ability to bounce back, whatever has happened.

- **Ties • Teams • Tribes**

We all need to be part of something bigger. Through giving you will consolidate and develop existing relationships and establish and shape new ones. These words said by Jesus (to be found in the Gospel of Matthew) say so much about the significance and power of partnership and collaboration: 'Again, truly I tell you that if two of you on earth agree about anything they ask for, it will be done for them by my Father in heaven. For where two or three gather in my name, there am I with them.'

- **Two**

'The Power of Two' lies in one-on-one mentoring – and in the potential for mentoring to work both ways. The Book of Ecclesiastes in the Bible takes this view on the Power of Two: 'Two are better than one, because they have a good reward for their toil. For if they fall, one will lift up his fellow. But woe to him who is alone when he falls and has not another to lift him up.'

- **Technology**

Technology continues to transform our lives and empower us. We can't live without it, and it holds all kinds of possibilities when it comes to giving, but we can never live – or give – entirely through technology. In the end, there is no substitute for face-to-face, hands-on action and interaction.

- **Trial**

Trial is about admitting that – as an entrepreneur in giving – you are not necessarily going to get everything right first time. It's also about taking a realistic and purposeful approach by projecting and planning your actions accordingly. Trial is about the process of learning and improvement and achieving the optimum result in the end.

- **Transmission**

Transmission is about passing on principles, ideas, learning and wisdom to other people. It is about helping other people to benefit from your experience (and that includes your mistakes as well as the things you got right). This doesn't mean that you are 'giving a lecture' or imposing your thinking – what other people take on board is up to them. And transmission gives you another opportunity to keep learning and growing. It's a process that can work both ways, becoming an exchange of knowledge and experience.

6

Trailblazing

When you unearth your talents, you are just at the start of your giving pilgrimage. It will take time, focus and effort to channel them into a talent for giving that you can apply and develop throughout your life.

At the heart of entrepreneurial giving is a constant process of discovery, interpretation and action, of challenge and success. As happens in life, you will sometimes experience failure too. But a setback or two – providing you learn from the experience – shouldn't prevent you from playing your unique role in making the world a better place. You might decide to lend your energies to innovating in an established organization, or you might prefer to take the independent route and launch your own projects and programmes. Whatever the case, entrepreneurial giving is about taking the talents you have unearthed, giving them a kickstart and applying them with some determination to an issue you feel passionate about.

There is always more to entrepreneurial giving than simply making a charitable donation or casually volunteering some time. It is about questioning or even challenging current practice. When you look at an existing organization, you need to ask: 'Does it have the resources and structures in place to solve the problems that are of special concern to me? Is it ready to start achieving the change I'd like to see?'

Entrepreneurs take a creative approach to problems and opportunities, but entrepreneurship is also about trading. Trading began as barter – giving someone something in return for receiving something back … 'I can use a little bit of yours, you can use a little bit of mine … We both benefit in the end.' In entrepreneurial giving your 'currency' is your talent. You apply it to an issue or an organization with the aim of changing the world for the better. If, with your help, an organization can rise to the demands you make on it, and if, with the organization's help, you start to succeed in your aims, you will benefit both as an individual and as a member of society. Some of those benefits might be intangible, but they are no less real for that.

When you are thinking about lending your talents to an organization, you should ask yourself: 'What do I bring to the table here? How does my talent complement or enhance this organization?' You don't want just to duplicate or reproduce its existing work. Being an entrepreneur isn't about 'more of the same'.

If you make an entrepreneurial approach to an established organization, you might find that it's not open to the particular talents you offer or the innovative ideas you put forward. Organizations have their own way of doing things and they are not always in a position to change.

If that's the case, you might have to go the fully entrepreneurial route and launch your own project or create your own organization. You won't be doing this to satisfy your ego and to show the world you can go it alone. It will be because you believe it is the best way of solving a problem you have identified – and because no one else seems to have come up with precisely the solution you have in mind. Essentially, you see your solution as a way to start changing the world one person at a time.

On my own journey through entrepreneurial giving, the fundamental driving force has been my belief in the primacy of human dignity. If I see that someone is being denied their share of human dignity, my sense of compassion is powerfully triggered. At the same time, even if I feel pity or outrage, I am buoyed by a 'glass-half-full' attitude to life. If I become aware of a problem that is crying out for a solution, my instinctive response is not to leave it to someone else: I take up the challenge myself.

Absolutely central to this ethos is my faith in God and its expression through my identity as a Catholic. Not everyone ascribes to a religious faith, but – as with our talents – we all need a particular ethos that feeds into our vision and our mission. By understanding it and defining it for ourselves, we can benefit to the full from the power that ethos holds.

There is a prayer written by St Teresa of Ávila in the sixteenth century that makes clear why, as a Christian, I feel such a strong personal responsibility for doing what I can to make the world a better place:

> Christ has no body now but yours.
> No hands, no feet on earth but yours.
> Yours are the eyes through which he looks compassion on this world.
> Yours are the feet with which he walks to do good.
> Yours are the hands through which he blesses all the world.
> Yours are the hands, yours are the feet, yours are the eyes, you are his body.
> Christ has no body now on earth but yours.

You and I share this earth with more than eight billion other human beings. Dignity should be the right of every one of them. That universal issue drives my entrepreneurial giving. On a purely personal level – and this has nothing to do with ideals or ideology – I am driven by my impatience. When it comes down to it, I like to seize the moment and get things done. I do my best to channel my impatience into positive action, and it helps that by nature I'm a convener: when I feel passionate about an issue, I can be very good at persuading people or organizations to lend their talents or devote their resources to dealing with it.

One of the Ts of entrepreneurial giving comes into play at this point, and that's temerity. Temerity is about being bold and upfront, not afraid to push at conventional limits when the moment is right. But sensitivity and strategic thought also have to come into play. If, eager to get people on board for a cause you believe in, the first bold thing you do is ask them for money, they might feel uncomfortable. It's better to start off by asking for advice, or for pointers to other people who might be able to help. You will be reassured and encouraged by just how generous people can be.

Talking of temerity, as a teenager in a small town in Massachusetts in the late 1960s, I found my way to setting up a toll-free telephone helpline for young people who had questions and concerns about sexually transmitted diseases. STDs were a taboo subject at the time and definitely not the kind of thing you discussed with your friends. Encouraged by one of my teachers, who helped me gain access to people with the right knowledge and connections, I established the helpline and the basic infrastructure to run it. It was manned by young volunteers who had been trained by a local public health nurse to answer callers' questions.

The helpline started off as a local service, but it represented what the business world calls a scalable model. Eventually, by tapping into existing networks and resources, we took the helpline across the entire USA. Key to gaining national traction was the support we elicited from the Jaycees – officially known as the United States Junior Chamber – a respected organization which develops leadership skills in younger adults. Not only did the Jaycees provide vital financial resources, it made a huge difference to have the organization's name behind us as we spread the word about our helpline.

I'm not telling you this to say, 'This is how it's done', and I'm not giving myself some kind of pat on the back. What I'm saying is, 'Look what it's possible to do with the help of some passion, determination and vision, and with some good advice from the right people.' It is up to you, as an entrepreneur in giving, to decide what you want to happen and how you make it happen. Each situation will be different, and it is up to you to 'read the room' and map out your path of action accordingly.

When I was in my twenties and my day job in finance had taken me to London, I became deeply involved with a totally different start-up project: The Passage, which was established in 1980 and has since become the UK's largest centre for homeless and insecurely housed people. At the instigation of Cardinal Basil Hume, who was then Archbishop of Westminster, The Passage, based near

Victoria Station, started life as a day centre for homeless people run by the Daughters of Charity, a group of religious sisters. They have been caring for the poor in Westminster for more than 150 years and can trace their existence to seventeenth-century France and the work of St Vincent de Paul, a committed 'servant of the poor' who is honoured in the name of Depaul UK, an organization that supports young homeless people.

The values behind The Passage have been consistent for 400 years, but it is very much a twenty-first-century organization, recognized as a leader in its field. In its early days I acted as a project manager and gofer, and since then I have remained a hands-on volunteer while also working to shape the charity's governance and bring new supporters on board. It means a great deal to me in my daily life to collaborate closely with its highly professional management team as we continue to realize Cardinal Hume's original vision.

Cardinal Hume (who died in 1999) was a great inspiration to me – I think of him as a mentor. He is indirectly responsible for the creation of the Genesis Foundation, which I formally established in 2001. The Foundation's core mission is to nurture the careers of exceptional young artists from a diversity of backgrounds.

In 1998, in celebration of Cardinal Hume's 75th birthday, I commissioned *Westminster Mass*, to be performed in Westminster Cathedral, the largest Roman

Catholic church in England and Wales. The composer was Roxanna Panufnik, then aged just 30 and building her reputation. (If I hadn't been in the fortunate position of being able to fund the commission myself, I would have found ways of raising the necessary funds to honour Cardinal Hume and Westminster Cathedral, and to give the world a new choral work.) The success of the Mass, its significance for Cardinal Hume and the Cathedral, and above all its ability to open numerous doors for Roxanna, encouraged me to think more about the potential for creative projects to produce multiple positive outcomes. I thought especially about young artists and their innate power to create the cultural memory of tomorrow. When Janet Suzman, the distinguished actress and director, told me that prospects for a creative career were becoming bleak for anyone not born into privilege, I realized that further action was necessary.

Thinking in terms of entrepreneurship, the Genesis Foundation grew from spotting a gap in the market: there was a need for an organization to nurture exceptional creative talent 'in the round'. It does this partly by offering funding and commissions to people who are aiming to make a living through their talent. So far so conventional. But it also takes a more innovative and distinctive approach by enhancing their access to the kind of knowledge, experience, infrastructure and professional networks that help them develop and sustain their careers in the long term. Over its existence the Genesis Foundation, built around a trusted nucleus of people with complementary talents, has helped to develop the careers of literally thousands of artists and creative professionals, enhancing their ability to make a long-term contribution to society through their work.

The idea for the Foundation grew from a piece of choral music, and one of its most fruitful relationships has been with Harry Christophers, founder and conductor of the world-renowned choral group The Sixteen. He and his singers have given numerous premieres of new sacred choral works commissioned by the Genesis Foundation. An initiative launched in 2011 and steered by Harry, the Genesis Sixteen training programme, has reinforced the skills, confidence and professional credentials of hundreds of outstanding young ensemble singers. Many of them have gone on to take an entrepreneurial approach to building their own careers and establishing performing groups, and, through encouraging public participation in music-making, to enriching communities.

Mentors and networks will always be important to me, and they matter in almost every walk of life. They represent a lifeline for creative professionals, who often have to take an entrepreneurial approach in developing and managing their careers. The principles of mentoring and networking formed the foundation of the Genesis programmes for young theatre professionals that were run by the Young Vic, a dynamic London-based institution with a strong national reach.

As I see it, the way everything fell into place for the Genesis Foundation was guided by the Holy Spirit. In purely earthly terms, the Foundation has benefited from its tight strategic focus, its capacity for anticipating change and adapting to circumstances, and its commitment to making optimum use of available resources.

Genesis puts firm structures in place, but they are not fixed or static. If you are entrepreneurial, you don't stand still and you retain flexibility and agility.

Over the years the Genesis Foundation has consistently piloted, tested and re-tested its models for mentoring, commissioning, grant-making, scholarships and the training programmes run in its name by trusted, dynamic, expert partners at leading arts organizations. We constantly monitor and review our activities. Sometimes, we see the need to prune projects or, when the time is right, to bring them smoothly to an end. These disciplines are all part of the entrepreneurial skillset – as is an ability to gain a multiple return on your investment.

Genesis invests in creative talent, and when Covid struck in 2020, bringing so much to a standstill, the Foundation created its Kickstart Fund. Grants were allocated to 95 arts projects around the UK with the aim of enabling more than 1,000 outstanding freelance artists to stay on their career paths despite the pandemic. The 'domino effect' of this initiative had major implications for the future of the creative industries in Britain.

That's told you something about my continuing journey through entrepreneurial giving, but how about yours?

In any field of endeavour, your journey as an entrepreneur will start with a desire to do things for yourself, to kickstart a process of change. It's worth bearing in mind that every great humanitarian movement and organization started with an individual. That one person identified a need and an opportunity for positive change and then had the courage, motivation and tenacity (another of those Ts) to get things off the ground.

The word 'entrepreneur' is especially linked with innovation in the world of business, and with movers and shakers in technology, but the entrepreneur's tools can be applied to any situation. When it comes to taking an entrepreneurial approach to giving, the competitive cut and thrust that matters so much in commercial activity is hardly top priority. All the same, you need to remain purposeful, determined to make an impact, and ready to question conventional wisdom. Keep your goal in sight and keep yourself ready to make the most of the opportunities and resources available to you.

Entrepreneurial giving is about being an agent of change – change for good, of course. Anyone who is looking to achieve constructive, sustainable change needs to question and challenge the state of the world – or at least the part of the world they can play some role in shaping. Entrepreneurship of any kind involves creative thinking, canny decisions and calculated risks. Whether those risks end up leading to the success or relative failure of any initiative, you must be ready to learn from your experience.

Entrepreneurs often talk about the 'freedom to fail', and the truth is that you can learn more from your failures than your successes. But you have to be ready to admit to those failures, recognize where you went wrong and do better – much better – next time. You might even have to reinvent the way you do things. No matter what you come up against, in your entrepreneurial giving your aim will be to achieve a multiple return on your investment of your talent and time, and, if it comes to it, on your investment of money (or treasure) too.

Through all this, your guiding forces will be your passion for changing the world, even in a small way, and the special talents you have defined for yourself. Whatever the scale of your ambitions, you will have some big thinking to do. Through thick and thin, your priority must be to take positive, purposeful action. When doubts are raised or obstacles arise, the entrepreneur will try a different route or something new. Simply giving up is an absolute last resort.

To ignite your entrepreneurial spirit, it will help to see yourself as an activist, as someone who has 'activated' their talents, who has it in them to create a movement. In fact, it matters more to think about activating talent than in a more abstract, generalized way about activism. That activation involves gaining people's trust and motivating them to take action and achieve common goals for the common good.

Agility comes into play here. There is even an element of Darwinism and survival of the fittest. The people who do best in any endeavour are the people who know their worth and understand what they are good at. Self-knowledge and self-belief are part of the package, but so is an ability to adapt and evolve when the going gets tough. Fundamentally, success grows from understanding the skillset that goes with your talents and using it wisely to achieve your aims. In the context of giving, you are not thinking just about your own 'survival' or progress, but about the survival, well-being and progress of your entire 'species' – in other words the common good.

In your efforts to be the fittest – and to thrive rather than simply survive as an entrepreneur – you will inevitably learn from mentors and other people and organizations you observe in action. Sometimes, you will wholeheartedly follow their example, but you should not be afraid to do things your own way.

Your talents, knowledge and experience matter here, but so do your passions, convictions and instincts. When you are considering new ideas and new opportunities, it can help to trust your intuition as well as your learning and common sense: successful entrepreneurs tend to know when something just feels right. Equally, they will listen when warning bells go off somewhere in their heads. They will be ready to take preventative or remedial action.

THINK ABOUT SOME TIMES YOU HAVE ACTED AS AN ENTREPRENEUR IN ANY PART OF YOUR LIFE – BY TAKING THE INITIATIVE AND DOING THINGS YOUR OWN WAY IN ORDER TO ACHIEVE A CLEARLY DEFINED AIM.

- What new talents did you unearth in the process?
- To what degree did you follow your passions? Did you question conventional wisdom? How much experience were you able to draw on?
- How much did your intuition come into play? How much temerity was required?
- How did it all work out for you?
- If you made mistakes, what did you learn from them?
- How could you apply what you learned to entrepreneurial giving?

I've mentioned temerity, but what exactly is its role – and the associated role of tenacity – in entrepreneurial giving?

An aspect of temerity is a readiness to challenge the status quo. There is a reason why entrepreneurs talk, in a positive sense, about being 'disruptors'. Inevitably, on your journey through entrepreneurial giving, you will run the risk of getting someone's back up. But if you really believe in something, that's a risk you should be prepared to take. Think of it this way: when you get someone's back up, you're getting them to think about a situation in a different way, whether they like it or not. The stimulus might even do them some good.

It will help your cause if your temerity goes hand in hand with respect and a constant awareness of what you are aiming to achieve. If you make it clear that you are working for the common good, people will be more likely to stay on your side.

Essentially, temerity is about not being afraid to ask. If you ask in the right way – making clear that you are reasonable as well as passionate, and that you are grateful for help – you won't compromise existing or future relationships. Obviously, you will be looking for a positive response – maybe even just a 'We'll think about it', 'We'll come back to you on this one', or 'Come and see us again in six months'. The worst that can happen is that someone will say 'no' to you. That might discourage you for a time, but it's not the end of the world.

This is where tenacity comes in. I always say that you might well have to knock on 19 closed doors before the 20th door opens for you. If you believe in what you are trying to achieve, you must be ready to consider alternatives, to investigate further options, to develop new and compelling arguments and to believe that any door might open to you. Polite persistence really can produce rewards. You will still have to steel yourself for hearing the word 'No', but the tenacious entrepreneur is always ready to ask again when the time feels right.

But how will you know if the time is right? As in so many things in life, it helps to have a plan with objectives, a schedule and allocation of resources. How you make that plan is up to you (and you probably know plenty of people who can help you with it), but it will be worth applying some rigour to your planning. This will certainly pay off by strengthening your case when you go knocking on doors. It's not as if giving is something you are approaching casually. It might be a voluntary activity for you, but you still mean business.

You will need to be flexible in your planning – that's part of both your realism and your entrepreneurial agility – and you should make space for regular reviews to track your progress, gauge your evolution, identify lessons you have learned, and pinpoint where you could do better. If all goes well you will create a virtuous circle as success boosts your self-esteem and motivates you to achieve still more.

In life as we live it, not everything goes to plan, but, whatever happens, the journey you take with your giving will expand your horizons. It will be up to you to use your talents to provide the kickstart and build your initial momentum. You're going to have to show some determination and persistence along the way, but entrepreneurial giving is about achieving results and achieving change – for you, for the people around you, and for the common good.

7

Common ground, common sense, common good

'It is prodigious the quantity of good that may be done by one man, if he will make a business of it.' That statement, though it was made almost 250 years ago, sums up the whole spirit of entrepreneurial giving. It was written in 1783 by an American in Paris – Benjamin Franklin. Over his long life Franklin made phenomenal use of his time and multiple talents, playing a hugely influential role as a successful businessman who was also a scientist and inventor, a journalist, social commentator and philosopher, and a diplomat and politician. As one of the Founding Fathers of the United States of America, he helped to draft the Declaration of Independence, a document he also signed.

You can see why Franklin has been described as the greatest polymath in American history.

He is even credited with popularizing the maxim 'God helps those who help themselves' – words that he clearly took to heart. From humble beginnings he became a highly successful entrepreneur as a printer, making enough money to retire at the age of 42. For the next 40 years he devoted his abundant energies to what he called the common good.

Franklin casts a huge shadow. A while ago I met Lin-Manuel Miranda, creator of the hit musical *Hamilton*, which tells the story of another Founding Father of the USA, Alexander Hamilton. I asked him why Franklin doesn't appear in the show. He replied: 'You couldn't put him in *Hamilton*. He dwarfs everybody – not just Hamilton, but Jefferson and Washington too.'

Maybe surprisingly, it wasn't by asserting himself as a dominant force that Franklin got to be so big. Instead, he did it by championing a collaborative approach – even if he was generally the person driving the thinking. He understood that together we are stronger, that we can achieve great things through co-operation, networks and pooled resources.

Rather than working as a lone activist, Franklin gained broader traction for his innovative ideas by channelling and amplifying them through like-minded groups of people. In 1727 in his adoptive hometown of Philadelphia, he established a 12-man 'club for mutual improvement' named the Junto. Each of its members was encouraged to put forward themes for discussion, covering 'Morals, Politics, or Natural Philosophy'. In due course the members of the Junto became co-founders of a pioneering public lending library – the first library of its kind in America, and probably the first in the world. The Library Company of Philadelphia, now an independent resource for research into American history, continues to serve the public today. For nearly 300 years its motto has remained the same, and as true as ever: *Communiter Bona profundere Deum est*, or 'To pour forth benefits for the common good is divine.'

Through his advocacy and activism Franklin fathered other public institutions in Philadelphia: a university, a hospital, a fire department and a police force. All of them broke new ground for the community and for society more widely. Nearly 30 years after the Library Company came into being, he put his thoughts in a letter to the Scottish philosopher David Hume. He wrote of 'a certain Interest too little thought of by selfish Man, and scarce ever mention'd, so that we hardly have a Name for it; I mean the *Interest of Humanity*, or common Good of Mankind.' We can be grateful to Benjamin Franklin for putting a name to it: the interest of humanity and the common good should matter just as much to us as they did to him.

Every American has a connection with Benjamin Franklin. In the early 2000s, as an American in London (and as an American who, like Franklin, came from Massachusetts), I had an opportunity to deepen that connection. I became involved with fundraising for a heritage project with an educational mission: the creation of a museum in the London house, a stone's throw from Trafalgar Square, where Franklin lived between 1757 and 1775. At the time he was serving as a diplomat for Pennsylvania. I'm happy to say that the house opened to the public on Franklin's 300th anniversary in 2006 and has since welcomed something like a quarter-of-a-million visitors – many of them children. Significantly, the 20th anniversary of the Benjamin Franklin House museum, which falls in 2026, coincides with the 250th anniversary of the USA's Declaration of Independence.

For all his historical stature, we still need to keep getting the word out about Franklin: his values, ideals and sense of purpose matter as much as ever.

When he was in his seventies, still looking to the future, he wrote: 'The rapid Progress true Science now makes, occasions my Regretting sometimes that I was born so soon. It is impossible to imagine the Height to which may be carried in a 1000 Years the Power of Man over Matter ... O that moral Science were in as fair a Way of Improvement, that Men would cease to be Wolves to one another, and that human Beings would at length learn what they now improperly call Humanity.'

Franklin speaks in the language of a distant era, but what he says holds as true as ever. The human race continues to make great strides in technology, art and science, but it fails to make similar progress in its 'moral Science'. Sadly, people continue 'to be Wolves to one another'. The world still has a lot to learn from Franklin and his enlightened, generous-spirited, but firmly grounded ethos. We all need to think about the 'prodigious quantity of good' that each of us can do. Like Franklin, we can further our cause by taking both an entrepreneurial and a collaborative approach as we 'make a business of it'.

If we are hoping to achieve something for the common good, we first need to identify and inhabit common ground. It's a matter of sharing space in our heads and hearts with other people who stand to benefit from our ideas and plans.

The easy part of this is to achieve an understanding with people who fundamentally think the way we do. It is more difficult to find some kind of harmony with people whose views we do not naturally share, and who might be sceptical about ours. When deep-seated passions and beliefs are at stake, it can be hard to find room for a different point of view, or even to identify the principles and opinions you already happen to share. But it pays to put some real effort into mapping out the common ground, sensitively but firmly.

In the third decade of the twenty-first century our efforts to find common ground are being hindered by a sometimes stubborn insistence on personal or group identity. This threatens to eclipse our shared and undeniable identity as members of the human race. Whatever else we do or is done to us, that human identity does not change.

We live in a time where people across the world are better connected than ever before, thanks to technology and transport systems. In principle, this should help bring us all closer together, and in many ways it does – over the last 50 years society has succeeded at least partially in overcoming some long-standing, deep-seated prejudices. Yet in some respects the world has never felt so fragmented, territorial and fractured. Individuals and groups resolutely define their patch and get defensive when anyone ventures into their zone – even if the approach being made is peaceable. It is reasonable and wise to set limits, but you cannot take things forward if you instantly build new barriers.

At least part of the reason for this state of affairs is the influence of social media, which has become such a force since Facebook was established in 2004 and Twitter (now X) in 2006. Social media requires comparatively little effort and minimal expenditure on our part. It is live 24 hours a day, it works with sometimes frightening speed and it can be addictive. If we want to get our message out to the world (or at least to the people in our particular online world) we no longer have to worry about the physical practicalities of setting up a soapbox or stuffing letters and flyers into envelopes and finding postage stamps.

When we're online, most of us don't think as carefully about our messages as we do when we're preparing a speech, a script or a report. But as we frantically type and fire off our posts, something crucial can get left by the wayside: the exchange of ideas that has built our civilization. In the online environment – which is not the real world, no matter how much time we spend in it – we can become fixated on shouting loudly and frequently. We just want as many people as possible to hear what we have to say.

Equally, in our online interactions we are at the mercy of algorithms, at danger of trapping ourselves in a digital echo chamber where nuanced debate is not on the agenda. In that echo chamber our impression can be that everything is a matter of 'them and us' – with 'us' being everyone inside the echo chamber and 'them' being everyone outside it. When that happens, we are denying ourselves even the possibility of seeking and finding common ground.

Of course, tensions and difficulties in communication are nothing new: they are part and parcel of the human condition. It is just that social media condenses them and sets them out flatly on a screen in front of us. In a way it dumbs them down, making them more inflammatory along the way. With all the knowledge and resources now instantly available to us, we really ought to be doing better when it comes to working towards the common good. Just think about three of the world's great religions – Judaism, Christianity and Islam. They represent well over four billion people and share origins and principles going back thousands of years, yet they are still so often perceived and (mis)understood in terms of their differences rather than their fundamental common ground.

Around 80 years before Benjamin Franklin was born, the English poet John Donne wrote:

> No man is an island,
> entire of itself;
> every man is a piece of the continent,
> a part of the main.

What he was saying is that we cannot exist in isolation, that we are all part of something bigger. The ground is by definition common.

If that is the case, we sometimes have to share at least part of our patch for the sake of the wider community. We might even have to share it with someone we don't feel in sympathy with. That should not, however, prevent us from coexisting with them in a civilized and mutually beneficial way. We all need to place our feet firmly on common ground and work together for the common good. If we find ourselves needing some further encouragement to take constructive action, we can turn yet again to one of Benjamin Franklin's sayings: 'Resolve to perform what you ought; perform without fail what you resolve.'

8

Trust is key

For a long time I saw the central Ts of giving as the triumvirate of time, talent and treasure. But as I thought further about the whole question of entrepreneurial giving, it became clear to me that there is a fourth T that belongs at the heart of the matter: trust.

No relationship can succeed without mutual trust. I'd go as far as to say that life is worthless without trust. In giving, trust plays an essential role in forming, strengthening and sustaining connections and in defining the relationship between the donor and the beneficiary. If you have something to give, there has to be trust between you and the direct beneficiary, whether that is a person or an organization.

The imperative for trust becomes still greater if your giving is driven by an entrepreneurial ethos. As an entrepreneur, you never stop questioning the status quo and moving with the times and circumstances. You thrive on relationships that evolve, welcoming opportunities for renewal and reinvention. But through all this, success in entrepreneurial giving has to remain rooted in firm, constant and unquestionable trust. Trust and respect go hand in hand. As a relationship develops and deepens over time, so does trust, but – and sadly we've all seen this happen – trust can also be undermined in an instant. It is something to be both treasured and nurtured, and something to be constantly earned.

The first person you have to trust – even before you start establishing your relationships for giving – is yourself. What, though, does it mean to trust yourself? It is a matter of understanding your motivations, of knowing what you want; of being able to read the dynamics of any particular situation, and of your chemistry with the people around you. You could call it confidence. That doesn't, however, mean arrogance: someone who has real confidence will know and admit when they didn't get something right and do their best to make sure things go better next time. They will also be ready to acknowledge when someone else has superior knowledge or better judgement.

Like any other form of trust, trust in yourself needs to be earned constantly – it's never a good feeling to let yourself down. Developing it can take some courage (or if we are talking Ts, temerity), but, as the saying goes, 'Nothing ventured, nothing gained.' If you're ever going to produce a return from your entrepreneurial investment of time, talent and treasure you'll need to trust yourself enough to put yourself out there. That means exposing yourself to some calculated risks. Going back to the Parable of the Talents, the third servant – the one who buried his boss's money 'safely' in the ground – betrays his boss's trust and betrays himself, all because he is afraid. He is no doubt intimidated by his boss, and when entrusted with money, doesn't have enough faith in himself to invest or trade. Ironically, it is his fear of failure that ends up causing him to fail.

If we learn how to trust ourselves, and how – and when – to trust other people, we gain a sense of security. Trust becomes the basis for respect and transparency, for empathy, for a sense of community, and for honest collaboration that gets the best out of time, talent and treasure.

In today's society – with its fake news, fake personas, skewed algorithms and 'real' images and sounds that turn out to be manipulated or AI-generated – our capacity for trust is increasingly challenged. Even your trust in yourself, your own eyes and instincts and your knowledge and experience, can be undermined by the unsettling, but insinuating messages you see and hear on social media. In this destabilizing environment, we urgently need real human contact, not just remote contact through a screen or a speaker. It is more important than ever to establish solid, trusting personal and professional relationships. Ideally these should be based on some good old-fashioned face-to-face discussion and actively nurtured and sustained over time. A relationship doesn't have to be 'love at first sight'. Your initial impressions matter, but you should be ready to put some thought and effort into someone you feel can inspire trust and who seems to hold the promise of value.

Key to building a trusting relationship is what I call the art of listening. Once again, it has to start with you.

First of all, you have to listen to yourself, so that you can understand yourself and believe in yourself while acknowledging your limitations. There is a lot to be said for confidence – it's very much part of the entrepreneurial approach – but, to put it bluntly, if you're too full of yourself, you have no room for other people. The most productive and satisfying relationships are built on give and take, and the whole concept of the common good grows from the principles of shared values, shared efforts and shared benefits.

It also grows from respect for other people's views, and being ready to listen to what they have to say, even if you are not coming from the same direction or actively disagree with them. When we listen to someone, our priority should be to learn and understand – not to come up with a response or a retort. It is through listening, learning and understanding that we gain in empathy.

Trust is built when you consciously give people time and space to share their thoughts. On occasion that might require some determination, and maybe even some silent gritting of teeth, but it is worth it if the result is a trusting relationship that works for everyone involved.

It can be daunting when you sense that someone is unlikely to want to agree with you. In my early days as a volunteer at the charity The Passage, it was clear to me that – understandably – some of the homeless people at the day centre saw me as a pushy young guy who spent his days with fat cats in the City of London. It wasn't just a matter of 'winning them round'. It was up to me to find common ground and establish trust.

One of the ways I did that was through active listening. For me, part of active listening is knowing when to ask questions, when to prompt someone else into giving voice to their thoughts, concerns and opinions. By asking your questions with both clarity and sensitivity, and by listening carefully and respectfully to the responses you receive – and by not leaping in to make points or argue your case – you can start to find common ground. Once you've found and marked out that common ground, you can start to build trust and a working relationship.

If there is an art to listening, it's an art that is becoming lost in the age of social media. It's hard to listen when your main worry is to get noticed, gain followers and get 'liked'. It pays to be selective in your listening – and it can take patience and tolerance to be someone else's audience – but by choosing *not* to listen you will miss opportunities to learn and grow.

Sometimes, rather than taking the lead, it is better to listen attentively and to wait to be asked for your view. Don't be afraid of moments of silence – they give you space and time. When you are listening, you are not taking a passive stance: listening plays an active part in building and nurturing relationships. At the end of a face-to-face discussion, which will always involve some careful listening on my part, I like to ask the other person if there is anything on their mind that we haven't talked about. I then leave a pause that they can choose to fill. That 'pregnant pause' can give birth to new possibilities and a new degree of trust.

As I said, there is nothing like being in the room with someone as you listen to them. It heightens your sensitivity not just to the words themselves, but to the way they are being said. What is being expressed in someone's body language? Is there a sense of conviction and passion? Are there suggestions of vulnerability or frailty? 'In the flesh' subtleties of that kind play a surprisingly large role in getting to know another person and in building trust. They can get entirely lost in remote or written communication. Hastily inserted, standard-issue emojis could certainly never do them justice.

The art of listening matters as much in the relationship between donor and beneficiary as in any other relationship. Most charitable giving happens from a distance, but entrepreneurial giving cannot remain at arm's length. It makes all the difference if you meet and get to know the people and organizations that stand to benefit from your giving.

Over the 40 or so years of my involvement with The Passage, I have never failed to gain something from working on the ground as a volunteer, especially at Christmastime. There are so many different reasons why people experience homelessness. When I meet a homeless person for the first time I go in without any preconceptions or expectations – for them or for me. It's a fresh start. Each of them has a unique story and they react and respond in their own distinctive way to me as a volunteer.

I will never forget a discussion I had one Christmas morning with a man who was letting his pride prevent him from phoning his estranged father. It was tough going, but I finally dialled his father's number for him and handed him the phone. That took some temerity on my part – I was taking a risk. For his part, he knew he was taking a risk in breaking the silence with his father. But he was also giving proof of trust – trust in me, trust in himself and, above all, a readiness to trust in his father. This was not about some kind of formalized relationship between donor and beneficiary, but about something very fundamental and human. We were all involved as equals and no single one of us was in control. I certainly never forget that we are all equal in the eyes of God.

Volunteering in some form can prove not just useful, but astonishingly powerful. It isn't about 'doing a favour', it is about investing your human capital in a particular purpose, project or programme. In the process you build trust between you and the organization to which you are committing your time, energy and talents. By volunteering in any capacity you are also giving yourself an opportunity to learn. If you are thinking in entrepreneurial terms, you will use your volunteering to identify opportunities too – how to do things differently and better, or on a more ambitious scale.

It's worth bearing in mind that a charitable organization is showing you trust by letting you, as a supporter or potential supporter, become a volunteer. You will be making a 'donation in kind', but you will also be acting as an observer, doing some research and digging about. Seeing things you might not see as an outsider, you will get the inside track on the charity's use of time and other resources. You will also gain insight into the experiences of its beneficiaries and how they respond.

If the charity in question is entrepreneurial in its thinking, it will take the opportunity to find out more about you too. On a formal level, it will do a safeguarding check, but my question here is whether the charity will actively seek to find out more about you – your motivation and values and how they match its ethos. If the chemistry is right, this could mark the start of a real, trusting, evolving working relationship.

One of the reasons I continue to volunteer as a helper at The Passage, decades after I played a part in founding the charity, is that it keeps revealing new facets to me. Not only that, but it gives me the opportunity to discover new facets of myself as I undertake various duties. As an organization The Passage continues to lead the way in its field, constantly adapting to meet and anticipate the diverse needs of people experiencing homelessness in London. I am proud of its work and happy that I'm still evolving with it.

In those early days at The Passage, when it was essentially a start-up, I was behaving as a young entrepreneur. In that capacity I was focusing less on the individual needs of each homeless person than on the 'business side' of the operation – its broader mission and strategy, its 'place in the market', its service model, its staff and recruitment, and its balance sheet. I also emphasized that everyone involved should treat the homeless people who came to The Passage as clients receiving a service rather than as beneficiaries receiving charity.

Over the years since then, I've taken a number of official roles at The Passage and have sat on its board of trustees. Today, what I continue to learn as a hands-on volunteer very much informs my more public voluntary activities for the charity, focused on awareness-raising and broadening and reinforcing the fundraising base. When I talk to people about The Passage, I want them to be able to have trust in every aspect of my experience.

Trust is built into the Genesis Foundation's working model, since the majority of the Foundation's funding goes to organizations that run programmes in its name, such as Genesis Sixteen, Genesis Almeida 'New Playwrights, Big Plays', the Genesis Music Theatre Programme at the National Theatre and the Genesis Future Curators Programme at the Royal Academy of Arts. These organizations are not just proven and prestigious forces on the UK's and the world's cultural scene, they have an ethos that marks them out for partnership with the Genesis Foundation.

At Genesis we believe in building durable relationships with teams we can trust. All our partner organizations are led by people who share our passions, and whose talents, vision, values and professionalism we respect. As far as we are concerned, that is our prerequisite for collaboration. Our partners put trust in us too, not simply in our role as providers of funding, but as people with a proven commitment to nurturing outstanding creative talent through distinctive programmes across a number of art forms. Along the way we have gained experience and wisdom while remaining open to innovative ideas. We still know how to listen! It is reassuring to feel that our partners can trust our judgement – and that after 25 years we continue to move with the times and retain our entrepreneurial spirit.

Central to the Genesis Foundation's ethos is the importance of mentoring and professional networks. Mentors and networks are influential and potentially transformative in anyone's life and career. They can certainly play a part in determining, fine-tuning and enhancing your practice of giving. I will talk about mentoring and networks in more detail in chapter 11, *The power of two*, but it goes pretty much without saying that trust plays an important role in both, along with the kind of astute judgement that blends intuition and rational thinking.

A trusting relationship is something to be treasured, but it can never be taken for granted. You have to keep gaining and earning other people's trust through your words and actions. Other people and charitable organizations have to keep earning your trust through theirs. Circumstances change, situations evolve, mistakes and crises happen – we are all only human – but if the mutual trust is there, and if the talent, the hard work and rigour are there, you can make entrepreneurial giving into a lifelong commitment.

9

The time of your life

The time you have on earth is your greatest gift from God. In turn, the greatest gift you can make to anyone is the gift of your time. It is within the power of every one of us to be generous with our time, but that doesn't mean we should give it away without thinking carefully. Time is our most precious resource and it is up to us to make the best use of it that we can.

We sometimes talk about having all the time in the world, but the truth is that we don't. We only have the time allotted to us and nobody knows exactly how much time that is. In saying that, I'm not being gloomy. I don't want to trigger thoughts like 'You only have one life,' or 'Life isn't a rehearsal.' And this is not the moment to start frantically putting together your bucket list. I just want to highlight how much we can give to the world – and how much satisfaction and joy we can gain – if we make purposeful use of the time we have. Rather than worrying about that bucket list of 'things to do before you die', you should be making a habit of asking yourself: 'Is this the best use of my time?'

I'll admit that sometimes I can be impatient – not impatient with people, but impatient for things to happen. Part of this probably comes from the fact that I was in a life-changing car accident when I was in my twenties. A crisis like that really changes your perception of the world and of what life – and living it to the full – is about.

If I sometimes seem impatient it's because I want to keep moving … learning, building relationships and doing the best I can. In fact, I want to keep getting better. That means I have to recognize and acknowledge my flaws before doing what I can to minimize them or compensate for them. But at the root of all this is my awareness of time as a gift from God. It is a privilege to have that time and I don't feel I have the right to waste it.

Time is precious, but that doesn't mean you should come out with a phrase we've heard all too often: 'Time is money.' That is a glib equation to make in the context of giving, and it's potentially destructive. Giving doesn't have to start with a quick financial calculation and a subsequent transaction. Nor should it end with it. There is always more you can do, and it comes down, above all, to making purposeful use of your time.

When you choose to devote some of your time to someone else – and not necessarily to someone you are close to – you are making a significant and positive gesture. By showing an interest in that person, exploring situations and possibilities with them, and taking the opportunity to apply some of your talents to their benefit, you are by definition showing that person respect. Both of you are also working on the assumption that you value each other's time. In other words, the respect is mutual. By devoting that shared time to a constructive end you are recognizing each other's dignity and value as a member of the human race.

In principle at least, giving your time is easy, but with life the way it is we all tend to feel pressure on our schedule. This makes the time we spend focused on someone else still more valuable. In even as little as 15 or 30 minutes – if those minutes are well-used and free of distracting attempts at multi-tasking – it is surprising and motivating to see how much you can achieve.

How often do you hear someone say something like 'I don't need to see him,' or 'I don't need to spend time with her'? This can sound reasonable enough, but it might also present a false picture of the situation. The real question is whether the other person feels it is important to spend some time with *you*. At any point, before you decide whether you 'need' to see someone, you should consider how much and why your time matters to them. For my part, I feel that if my time can be valuable to someone else, it is my duty to share it. What I don't need is people feeling they must spend time with me to 'keep me happy'. What makes me happy is being able to spend time doing something that will make a positive difference to someone else's life.

My life tends to be pretty full, and I believe in keeping as close as possible to a prepared schedule. My entire day, which usually starts early, is mapped out in advance – and that covers time for work, for travel, for volunteering, for social engagements, for exercise, and for prayer and meditation. It requires rigorous management, but, as I've said, time is the most precious gift we have. We need to make sure that everything gets the time it deserves: we should see every commitment we make as a first-class commitment.

When I've scheduled in time to volunteer at The Passage day centre in London, I know that just by spending half an hour with a homeless person I can do something to improve their frame of mind. If, following those 30 minutes, they feel better for just a few hours, that is already a meaningful return on my investment of time.

I won't just make chit-chat or small talk. Equally, I won't drive any agendas or look to teach any lessons. There are occasions when I feel it's best simply to offer company as a quiet presence. We live in a noisy world where we need to make room for silence; it isn't always necessary to make conversation. What matters is that my time, and the respect I'm expressing by being in the room, can be valuable to someone who might be in danger of feeling disconnected and isolated.

It is even possible that in the course of that half an hour I will give them something – an idea, a pointer, an answer or a piece of encouragement – that remains with them for the rest of their life. This is not because I'm some kind of whizz therapist or guru. It's because I show genuine interest, ask questions and engage fully and sincerely in conversation.

One of the points I make most frequently – to people in all walks of life – is that we often need to show patience and tenacity before things start to work out the way we want them to. We can't expect to get everything right first time – or even second or third time. We have to keep trying and we can hope to gain some wisdom along the way. I like to think that the timetable we end up following is the one that God has set for us.

Maybe surprisingly, that half-hour exemplifies aspects of entrepreneurial giving: over the course of that brief period you can find yourself leaving your comfort zone. Entrepreneurs make a habit of looking beyond the familiar. You can take up the challenge of spending time one-on-one with a person you hardly know, and who hardly knows you, and whose life has turned out very differently from yours. Your capacity to give relies on your ability to cross any perceived divides on either side and make the right kind of connection. Even if there are some awkward moments, the chances are that you will come out feeling better at the end of those 30 minutes. When you succeed in making a real connection, the energy flows both ways. You will learn something about yourself. You could even find yourself gaining a new life skill. The act of giving, in any form, can be very life-affirming, even exhilarating.

In our daily routine we all do our best to manage our time, but we always run the risk of 'giving in' to time and letting it manage us. If we lead busy lives, our days can become so filled with technology and logistics that we feel we have no time left for other people – never mind ourselves. If we manage to have some relative downtime, we can find the hours slipping by almost unnoticed and we end up wondering where they have gone.

This probably sounds obvious, but we can empower ourselves in our relationship with time by allocating a defined period to each activity (or period of inactivity) we foresee for our day. This doesn't always mean sticking rigidly to the allocated minutes or hours, but nor do you want to give time the upper hand by 'drifting'. If you want a firm sense of the time available to you and how you are making use of it, it helps to be conscious of an endpoint as well as a starting point.

You can empower yourself further through an awareness of the need to be 'present' at any moment. 'Being present' is a phrase that gets thrown around frequently, but for me it means living consciously and responsibly in the moment, focusing on what you are doing and on your interactions with the people around you. There are other times when you can (and should) make space to look back to yesterday or forward to tomorrow, but being present means *living* in the present.

Living in the present can sometimes be tough, but it's part of life as an entrepreneur to face challenges and to find ways of surmounting them. Your relationship with time plays a part in this, and there is a sentence in the Gospel of Matthew that offers some valuable advice on the approach to take: 'Therefore do not be anxious about tomorrow, for tomorrow will be anxious for itself. Sufficient for the day is its own trouble.' Don't overburden yourself with worries about the future, but focus on tackling the matters in hand.

Looking at the present in a very positive sense, you are never going to have this moment again, so why not experience and use it to the full? It could stand you in good stead. By the way, technology does not have to be part of the moment – or intrude on it. Our mobile phones have made us obsessed with the idea of capturing every event with a photo or a video, of being able to 'replay' moments in our life as a kind of meme. But the truth is that each moment in life only happens once. If, in that moment, you are giving of yourself fully to the people around you, you will be making the most of yourself and the most of them. Those 'fully present' moments soon add up. You will generate more energy and achieve more in a limited time than you might ever have imagined.

How much you achieve is also contingent on the talents you bring into play at any time. I said earlier that we should not give our time away indiscriminately. If you do that, you will end up wasting your time and other people's time too. Life is always about making choices and there is no more fundamental and important choice than how you use your time. Once you have made a choice and committed to it, it always pays to keep track of the way your time and talents are being used and of the impact you are making. When it all comes together and adds up to more than the sum of its parts, and above all when you are seeing and *feeling* results, the effect is energizing. Boosted by this extra energy, you will find yourself in a virtuous circle, able to bring still more to your projects and to the people around you.

Sometimes, though, no matter how hard you've tried and how many hurdles you might already have overcome, there comes a point where you must ask yourself: 'Is this best use of my time? … Could the time that I'm devoting to this project be used to greater effect elsewhere?'

In saying this I'm not questioning the value of tenacity (another of the Ts of entrepreneurial giving), especially when the going gets tough. It's no good being a quitter. All the same, a canny entrepreneur knows when an investment (of time or anything else) is no longer producing adequate returns. This does not of necessity mean that a project has failed. Sometimes, you will just have reached the point where you have done what you can, where your talents and time have been put to good use, and you can quite legitimately stand back and hand over to someone with a different set of talents and skills.

There's an analogy from the world of business. An entrepreneur will classically spot an opportunity in the market and then establish and build a business to exploit that opportunity. But that entrepreneur is not necessarily the best person to lead the business once it has settled into some kind of routine. Of course, some entrepreneurs also turn out to be brilliant line managers, but we all owe it to ourselves – and, indeed, to the world – to focus on the things in life that make best use of our time. When it comes to taking leave of a project, the implications of what you say and do can be just as great as when you took it on. Your responsibilities don't disappear entirely when you're ready to say goodbye.

The whole principle of making good use of my time was instilled in me when I was a young child. At the age of six or so my mother encouraged me to spend a few hours a week helping out in a community kitchen, distributing meals to people in need. Though I was very happy to be there, I was also terrified of messing things up, of being seen as 'just the little kid'. So I practised and practised at pouring soup neatly into a bowl. Even today, when I'm helping out at The Passage, I'm pretty good at ladling soup dead-centre with no splashes.

When you are a child, you have so much time ahead of you and you are so naturally receptive to new stimuli, new ideas and new experiences. Learning to devote time to other people and the community should be like learning to ride a bicycle: you might need a push to start you off, it might be a little scary at first, you might fall off a few times and suffer a few scratches, but the secret is to go with the flow. Once you get it right it will quickly take you to new places and you won't ever forget how it's done. Learning how to ride a bike is something that children tend to do when they are out of school, but maybe the official school curriculum should include lessons on using and giving time.

Teachers, like parents, have a determining role to play in channelling children's talents and passions into making the world a better place, and in opening their eyes to such concepts as humility, mercy, justice, generosity and responsibility. Taken together, concepts of that kind add up to a moral code to guide our actions and interactions in life. In our society moral codes often become identified with the principles of organized religion, but a formalized set of rules is not going to stimulate children in their understanding of God. It is better for them to learn and discover for themselves, above all through giving, and through making unselfish use of their own gifts – their talents.

For adults as well as children, the world is wondrous in so many respects, but for us as human beings it will always be imperfect. In the Book of Ecclesiastes in the Bible there is a reflection on time that goes some way to explaining how we fit into the greater scheme of things.

> For everything there is a season, and a time for every matter under heaven: a time to be born, and a time to die; a time to plant, and a time to pluck up what is planted; a time to kill, and a time to heal; a time to break down, and a time to build up; a time to weep, and a time to laugh; a time to mourn, and a time to dance; a time to throw away stones, and a time to gather stones together; a time to embrace, and a time to refrain from embracing; a time to seek, and a time to lose; a time to keep, and a time to throw away; a time to tear, and a time to sew; a time to keep silence, and a time to speak; a time to love, and a time to hate; a time for war, and a time for peace.

If we take an entrepreneurial approach to life those lines are also a reminder to take ownership of whatever time we can. While they suggest that time dictates the structure for your life, you can choose to see them as a reminder to take charge of your life. You can make time serve your purpose, every hour, every day, every week, every month, every year. Though it doesn't appear as one of Ecclesiastes' 'matters under heaven', it should matter deeply to you to find your own special time for giving.

10

Hunting for buried treasure

Talk to someone about 'giving' and their first thought might well be 'money'. But – and I've said it before and I'll say it again – giving is about much more than money. In fact, giving doesn't have to be about money at all. When it comes to being entrepreneurial, we all have other things to give away that can prove even more valuable.

We all like to think we understand about money, but – coming to another of those Ts on my entrepreneur's list – how well do we understand *treasure*? Only when you enrich it with time and talent does money become treasure. That process of transformation opens up new possibilities and wider horizons.

Let's go back to the Parable of the Talents. We see the first two servants winning their boss's approval by achieving financial gains on his behalf. Their success doesn't just happen by itself. It comes from applying some time, thought and business savvy to the money he has entrusted to them. There is some temerity involved too: the two servants are taking a risk here. In seeking to make a profit, they could end up losing the money if they don't call the right shots. What matters in the parable is that, with the aim of giving their boss a decent return on his money, they make the necessary investment of time and talent. Another of the Ts, trust, also comes into play. The boss shows his trust for his three servants by putting his money in their hands. In turn, to make any kind of profit, the servants need to put their trust in trading partners – they don't make the profit all on their own. ('Then he who had received the five talents went and traded with them, and made another five talents. And likewise he who had received two gained two more also.')

The first two servants take an entrepreneurial approach and enjoy some success. By contrast, the third, over-cautious servant applies virtually no time and absolutely no talent to the money entrusted to him. Nor is he ready to put any trust in a trading partner. He isolates himself and does nothing with the money beyond burying it and attempting to conveniently forget about it.

By simply giving money to charity you are, in a way, conveniently forgetting about it. You can click the 'Pay' button and get on with your day. With a single neat transaction your donation is out of the way and now you can leave the charitable work and the worry to someone else. In a way, it's a lazy option, though hopefully a safe one. If your money is going to a reputable, well-run charity that knows what it's doing, it's reasonable to assume it will be put to good, purposeful use. How often, though, do you actually follow up on what is happening to money you've donated?

Maybe you need to think about it differently. What if you consciously and actively applied your time and talent to making sure that your money is being put to *best* use – not just to good use? That would require an entrepreneurial approach – and my belief is that there is an entrepreneur to be unearthed in nearly all of us.

The secret lies in seeing money as more than something merely transactional – more than 'I give you this and I get this back.' Think about it. When you make a donation to a charity, what exactly are you getting back? Is it the reassurance that you are doing some good for the world? Or that you have scored a couple of points in your favour for that distant moment when you're waiting anxiously for admission at the Pearly Gates? Are you doing it because you feel pressure to live up to the expectations of people around you? Or are you simply hoping for relief – probably temporary – from feelings of guilt? Or, to see it from a more positive angle, has the charitable transaction given you an opportunity, in a complex, competitive and sometimes cruel world, to remind yourself how blessed you are?

This is where it makes a big difference to start thinking about *treasure* rather than simply about money. Treasure goes beyond a transaction. Money achieves its greatest value when time and talent play their part in turning it into treasure. Through its transformation into treasure, money attains its full and true worth. In turn, it becomes transformational.

When you donate money to a charity, you're leaving it to the people at that charity to put their time and talent into effecting that transformation. If you commit to entrepreneurial giving, you will devote your own time and talent to the causes and projects that really matter to you. As you put your ideas and plans into action, you will be the one who is generating and applying the transformational force.

We've talked about unearthing your talents, making sure that they come to light and don't go to waste. When it comes to treasure, you need to make sure it doesn't remain buried. If treasure is buried, its value remains unreleased. We're back with the third servant in the Parable of the Talents, who says, 'And I was afraid, and went and hid your [his boss's] talent in the ground.' If you summon up some bravery (or temerity), if your aims are clear, and if you can rely on solid, trusting relationships, you will release the value of treasure. As an entrepreneur you will steward your treasure with enthusiasm and energy, but always with a sense of purpose and responsibility.

'What goes around comes around.' We've all heard that expression, and it applies to treasure too. When you activate your money through well-judged use of time and talent, the treasure it becomes is an all-purpose currency. Transcending a single transaction, this currency proves its worth time and time again, circulating around the community, serving a diversity of good purposes, and building and sustaining relationships. When invested as treasure for the common good, your money multiplies its worth and compounds its value. You can give money away, but once it is circulating as treasure and working for the common good, you will find yourself pocketing a profit along with other members of society.

Since I established the Genesis Foundation 25 years ago my 'profit' lies in the way my life is enhanced by the achievements of creative professionals whose careers Genesis has nurtured. The lives of many thousands – even millions – of other people have been enhanced by their achievements too. There is no question in my mind that the work of artists and other creative professionals has a beneficial influence on society as a whole. On a more philosophical level they play a role in creating the cultural memory of the future. In the here and now, their work also enhances our well-being through enhancing our prosperity: the UK government estimates that in 2022 the country's creative industries generated £126 billion in value added to the economy. That is the quantifiable output for our society, but what about the kind of input that sets the whole creative process in motion? Money is just one of its components.

Since 2001, always with multiple returns in mind, the Genesis Foundation has invested some £25 million in thousands of outstanding creative professionals, most of them in the crucial early stages of their careers. In all the Foundation's programmes the transformative potential of that money is increased through partnerships with outstanding individuals and organizations who invest time and talent in training, mentoring and opening up professional networks. That's what I mean by turning money into treasure. This treasure holds long-term value for creative professionals as they go on to make a contribution to society through their work. They do this through channelling their creativity into projects, but also, in turn, through mentoring and networking – by sharing what they have learned with their peers and with people entering their professional sphere.

Of course, talent – creative and artistic talent – is the focus of the Genesis Foundation, but it takes time and talents of other kinds to develop it. Management skills take their place beside creative skills and mentoring skills in the Foundation's endeavours. Talking of time, the Foundation commits to funding programmes for a minimum of two years. Transformations of the kind we are talking about do not happen instantly and it takes time for even the best thought-out programme, staffed, steered and monitored by the highest-calibre people, to fine-tune its activities and find its feet before it fully hits its stride.

One of the Genesis Foundation's longest-established programmes is Genesis Sixteen, which I've already mentioned. Each year it offers intensive training for an annual intake of 25 or so classically trained choral singers (aged between 18 and 23) from around the UK and Ireland. The singers benefit from group tuition, individual mentoring, masterclasses and performance opportunities, and the programme is personally led by Harry Christophers, the founder and conductor of The Sixteen choir – long recognized as one of the world's leading vocal ensembles. Through the funding provided by the Genesis Foundation, the courses are provided free of charge to the young singers, and the people who run and staff the programme with such professionalism are paid for their time and expertise. Many of the alumni of Genesis Sixteen – there are now over 300 – have gone on to busy careers as professional singers, whether as members of choral groups or as soloists, bringing music to church congregations and concert audiences in the UK and around the world. Some have followed Harry

Christophers' example by taking the entrepreneurial route of founding their own ensembles, often with colleagues they met through Genesis Sixteen, and generating work for themselves and for other people. Others have gone on to run high-profile educational and community projects that draw in and inspire thousands of members of the public, of all ages. This shows what can happen when money, energized and enlivened through time and talent, is transformed into treasure. It becomes a new kind of currency, assuming multiple forms and producing multiple benefits.

Essentially, if you see money in isolation, it can limit its potential for doing good – and your potential for doing good too. This is not to say that 'throwing money at it' – in a well-targeted fashion, at least – has no place. As I've suggested before, charity can be about relieving immediate pain, applying an urgent 'sticking plaster' to a wound.

For example, in July 2020, during the first wave of the Covid-19 pandemic, the Genesis Foundation distributed £100,000 in emergency funding to freelance artists and creative professionals associated with the programmes run in its name by the Almeida Theatre, National Theatre, Young Vic, the drama school LAMDA and The Sixteen. As a result of the lockdown, these people's work had dried up and they needed help with basic living expenses. My decision to provide emergency funding to them through the Genesis Foundation was intuitive – as entrepreneurial decisions sometimes are. As far as I was concerned, there was no option. I knew that it was a short-term solution, but I saw that it had long-term implications too, since it would help ensure the recipients' future professional survival.

This emergency initiative also became the stimulus for the launch of a much larger funding programme several months later, still under pandemic conditions: the Genesis Kickstart Fund, which provided £1 million in grants for enterprising creative projects that employed freelance creative professionals. The fund was explicitly conceived to help these freelancers keep firmly on their career path. When the Foundation followed up with the freelancers in 2022, once all the projects had been completed, 94 per cent of them said that their Genesis Kickstart had helped them stay on track with their career at a time of crisis. Since the Kickstart Fund helped generate work for 1,000 self-employed people, that's a significant and substantial result – and something to be treasured.

The chances are that you as an individual won't be thinking of donating £100,000 to an emergency project. But however much or however little you give – and even if you're sticking for the moment with conventional charitable giving – you should avoid being a 'sleepwalking' donor. Entrepreneurs are not sleepwalkers. Make sure you know, as far as you can, where your money will be going and what it is likely to achieve. Do your research into the charity in question, and possibly even offer your time and talent as a volunteer if you feel passionate about its work. Quite apart from anything else, volunteering – a donation 'in kind' – is a great way of finding out what drives an organization and how it functions.

If a charitable organization makes a personal approach to you as a possible donor, think about the implications and be ready to ask yourself – and the charitable organization – some questions. (Maybe a little temerity needs to come into play here …) Are they talking to me about an emergency need or about 'business as usual'? Clearly this will affect the criteria you apply to their request. Do they see me in the round as a person, as someone with talents to contribute as well as money? How does what they say and do chime with my passions and convictions? … Do they seem interested in building a relationship with me? Do they want me simply as a passive supporter or am I being invited to make an active contribution through participation? Do they want to have me as a member of their organization? … How would I fit in with and complement the other members? What, beyond money, might I have to contribute to this organization?

What it comes down to is that ideally a charitable organization should understand that its donors represent human capital, not just financial capital. The essence of human capital lies in talent and time and in building trusting and responsible relationships. No matter how much money is involved, unless those Ts – talent, time and trust – are brought into play, the real treasure could remain buried forever.

11

The power of two

It would make a major difference to our lives – and to the world – if we all chose to spend more of our time alone with just one other person.

You don't even have to spend that time with someone who is already very close to you, such as a partner, sibling, parent or dear friend. There is so much you can discover about anyone – and about the world – from being one-on-one, exchanging impressions, opinions, ideas and knowledge in an honest and open way. Sometimes, you don't even need to talk: you can stay quiet, just sensing and respecting each other's existence. It's all about what I call the Power of Two. In our efforts to make the most of our time, talent and treasure, and to learn the truths of giving, nothing better demonstrates the Power of Two than the act of mentoring.

The central structure of giving is formed by time, talent and treasure, bound together and enriched by trust.

Fundamentally, our lives are ruled by time, though we always retain some freedom of choice as we find ways to fill the minutes and hours that God has given us. Talent and treasure, and our success in applying them, play a determining role in our existence. Whatever we do, the three Ts will loom large – so large that it takes more than informed instinct, accumulated experience, and a capacity for nurturing trust for us to make best use of them.

Giving is just one area of our life where we need to strike the right balance between time, talent and treasure as we respond to particular events, demands and opportunities. That balance is always crucial. Sometimes it is also delicate. At any moment in our evolution we might need some help in finding it, and in defining the place and space that each T occupies in our portfolio for giving. An entrepreneurial approach is about believing in ourselves and our talents – remaining true to our motivations and beliefs, and doing things our own way. But we should never stop being ready to invite and welcome sound guidance. This is where mentoring, the Power of Two, comes in.

Mentoring is an act of generosity, and it is first and foremost about being generous with your time. It can also turn out to be one of the best ways of using your time in the cause of the common good. Its essence, as it is generally understood, lies in a sustained one-on-one relationship and the transfer of knowledge and know-how from a 'senior partner', the mentor, to a 'junior partner', the mentee. At some point in our life we've all been mentored, and at some point we've also all acted as a mentor, even if our role wasn't consciously or explicitly defined in those terms.

It's worth looking back on the important moments in your life and identifying the occasions when you met someone who went on to take responsibility for your development. Equally, you should think about times when you 'talent-spotted' someone, or when someone came to you for advice and support, and you helped them on their way.

When we use the term 'mentoring' it can sound like a formal commitment, almost like some kind of educational programme for which both participants must sign up. Mentoring can certainly work that way – there is no doubt that agreed structures can help us in making best use of our time – but it can also unfold informally, naturally and organically, simply in the normal course of things. It's possible that you might find yourself in a mentoring relationship without realizing it. There is nothing wrong with that, provided the relationship is respectful and trusting, and fruitful for both of you. In fact, you could say that the give and take of any worthwhile relationship embraces mentoring in some form.

I feel strongly that nothing beats face-to-face mentoring, with the mentor and mentee physically in the same place.

That being said, I'd like to think that this book represents a form of mentoring too. Admittedly, you and I probably won't have the opportunity to discuss our experiences and exchange our thoughts one-on-one, but I hope that the words you find here can 'speak' to you personally and feed into your life, stimulating and informing both thought and action. And, for me, the process of writing this book has definitely been about 'take' as well as 'give'. I've learned a lot as I've considered and reconsidered the principles and practices of giving, and specifically of entrepreneurial giving, and as I've done what I can to give them expression.

Like any successful relationship, a mentoring relationship works both ways. As the Book of Proverbs in the Bible puts it, 'Iron sharpens iron, and one man sharpens another.' It is not only the mentee who has something to gain. By acting as a mentor, you can acquire new insights into familiar situations and processes and hone your abilities in communicating ideas and providing motivation. Not least, you will learn from seeing aspects of life through your mentee's eyes.

No two people duplicate each other entirely in their talents. An element of complementarity will always come into play in mentoring, and it should be welcomed and encouraged. A significant overlap between the lives of the mentor and mentee is not indispensable: what matters are the mutual interests and the mutual ground that are relevant to your shared experience of mentoring. It is worth mapping these out at the beginning of the relationship.

Ideally, the relationship between mentor and mentee will be reliably harmonious, but that doesn't mean that you should both feel obliged to be in agreement on absolutely everything. If you both come from entirely the same direction and concur on every point, you run the risk of creating a well-meaning 'echo chamber'.

We have quite enough echo chambers in our lives already – I mean the ones produced by algorithms on social media, working on the principle that 'If you like that, you'll like this …' Echo chambers not only prove limiting, they can even prove damaging if the reverberation drowns out some vital home truths. A mentoring relationship is built on honesty and, if the circumstances are right, the mentee should feel at liberty to question the mentor's wisdom. The mentor, meanwhile, should be ready to take that questioning with a generous spirit and to see it as an opportunity to view things afresh. A few differences of opinion might introduce some passing tension into the relationship, but they can give rise to very fertile discussion and take both mentor and mentee somewhere new. Both of you will stand to learn something from the exchange of ideas. As another line says in the Book of Proverbs, 'Whoever walks with the wise becomes wise …'

But it is not necessarily a case of 'older and wiser'. Mentoring doesn't have to be a matter of a more mature person 'taking charge' of a younger person. Conventional hierarchies, like conventional wisdom, can get in the way. A baby boomer with an open mind can have their understanding transformed by a digital native of Generation Z.

Peer-to-peer mentoring can also prove very fruitful. If the context and chemistry are right, anyone of any generation should be ready to act as a mentor to someone of similar age and a similar level of experience. In a mentoring relationship receptiveness and humility matter on both sides, along with a readiness to admit to vulnerabilities. You shouldn't be ashamed to recognize and flag up past or current chinks in your armour or gaps in your portfolio or toolbox.

Mentoring is built on talking, listening – the art of listening really comes into play here – advising, counselling and, in the true sense of the word, sharing: you will both take something away with you. When you act as a mentor, taking time to share your ideas and wisdom, you enhance and enlarge your mentee's skillset by tapping into their talents and potential. A good mentor won't tell their mentee exactly what to do, but, after some careful listening, will draw on their experience and lay out options within a rational framework.

Sometimes, as a mentor, you will find yourself showing a mentee where they have been going wrong – that is part of the deal in responsible mentoring – but the flipside of that is that you will point the way to solutions. One of your aims is to save your mentee fruitless trial and error, which, if not handled confidently, can waste time, talent and treasure and eat away at trust.

As the self-help gurus say, you are supplying your mentee with 'life hacks'. Only here we are not talking about the kind of glib, standard-issue tips you read about on the Internet or access through an app. A mentor offers individually tailored advice and guidance, based on personal insights and passed on from one person to another within the framework of a sustained, trusting, generous relationship. If we are thinking about the kind of 'hacks' for giving that a mentor would supply, they are not focused solely on maximizing impact more rapidly and efficiently, but also on maximizing impact with greater awareness, depth and meaning.

Mentoring is, of course, in itself a form of giving. To echo the point I made earlier about philanthropy and charity, mentoring is about more than giving a man a fish so that he won't go hungry today. It's about teaching a man *how* to fish – so that he won't go hungry tomorrow or the day after that. Real mentoring is about sustainability rather than a quick fix, though quick fixes (and figurative sticking plaster) have their place in an emergency. When I devote time to mentoring, whether with an ambitious young businessperson, an emerging artist, or a homeless person who is working at putting their life back together, my aim is both to be supportive in the moment and to play a part in building my mentee's long-term resources.

As I've already implied, age is just a number when it comes to mentoring. We can all draw strength from mentoring relationships with different people at different stages of our lives. Equally, we can have different mentoring relationships for different areas of interest and endeavour. I'm not suggesting that you should spread yourself thin – true mentoring requires commitment, a strong focus and a sense of dedication and specificity – but there is nothing to stop you having more than one mentee (or mentor) in your life.

If you feel you would benefit from mentoring in a particular area of your life, you can actively identify, seek out and approach someone about becoming your mentor. We should all be ready to seek mentors, just as we should all be open to mentors seeking us. When it comes to giving, at any stage of your life you should be ready to ask yourself, 'How can I do more?', or 'How can I make a contribution?' With the help of a little temerity – that other, secondary T of giving – you can take yourself further by soliciting some good advice on finding the right answers.

As a first step, you could ask someone you respect and admire for 20 minutes of their time. This might be someone you don't know personally, but someone you've read or heard about. To provide focus and a clear starting point, you should suggest a specific topic for your discussion. If those 20 minutes go well, you could find them growing into a regular appointment.

On the other hand, your request for a chat might get turned down, but you shouldn't let that possibility prevent you from trying in the first place. To put it in hard-nosed terms, 'If you don't ask, you don't get.' Bearing another T in mind – tenacity – you can always try asking again after a suitable interval. If, at the first, second or third attempt, you make it through to seeing a prospective mentor, remember to leave them feeling that you are worth their time and endorsement, that you stand to reward the faith you hope they will place in you.

On the other side of the mentoring equation, if you agree to become someone's mentor, you must be ready to take responsibility for your mentee – at least within the scope of your mentoring relationship. It is a matter of inspiring confidence while remaining empathetic, of being sensitive to your mentee's vulnerabilities as much as to their strengths. You will need to be ready to guide them firmly through any rough patches they encounter. This whole dynamic, and much of the Power of Two, is summed up in the Book of Ecclesiastes: 'Two are better than one, because they have a good reward for their toil. For if they fall, one will lift up his fellow. But woe to him who is alone when he falls and has not another to lift him up.'

As a mentor, at times you will be called upon to act as a troubleshooter. At other times you might have to inject new motivation into a worthwhile project that's stalling for some reason, or to deflect (or even catch) a curve ball that's been thrown at your mentee. In different circumstances you might be expected to play policeman or provide professional scrutiny. Sometimes, mentoring might come down to simply applying your instincts, intelligently and responsibly – and no one in the world has exactly the same instincts as you.

Another of the T's of giving comes into play when we are talking about the Power of Two, and that is 'ties' – in other words, connections and networks, as crucial to success in giving as in every other endeavour. As a mentor, not only will you build close ties with your mentee but you can also release their potential by aiding their access to your networks. In doing this, you are setting a generous example for your mentees to follow in the future. Through these actions you are compounding and multiplying the Power of Two. As your networks branch out and branch off, and as your mentee's networks do the same, the composite network for mentoring and giving will grow exponentially. The implications of a single mentoring relationship can extend both far and wide.

Mentoring is very much part of the ethos of the Genesis Foundation – it's one of the ways we nurture the careers of outstanding artists and creative professionals. We've all heard people say that success in your career is not so much about what you know as who you know. The Genesis Foundation believes that if a talented person is determined to know more about their craft and profession, they will benefit hugely from getting to know a good mentor. The mentor might be called upon for creative insight or technical expertise, for encouragement and reassurance when there are big decisions to be made, or for sound advice and useful connections when opportunities or difficulties arise.

The Genesis Foundation ensures that mentoring is a pillar of the professional training and development programmes run in its name by such cultural and arts institutions as London's National Theatre and Royal Academy, the Jewish Literary Foundation and the choral group The Sixteen. These are creative organizations acknowledged for their expertise in a particular area and they can be trusted with identifying exceptional talent and with knowing how to support and develop it.

Part of their creativity lies in knowing how to innovate without compromising their essential identity and heritage. As a partner to these organizations, the

Genesis Foundation brings insight and experience built up over 25 years of funding, fuelling, shaping, monitoring, energizing and sometimes re-engineering projects, programmes and networks. Genesis, with its entrepreneurial mindset, continues to evolve and learn, above all through its partnerships. Equally, Genesis's partners recognize the value of the distinctive perspective and knowledge that the Foundation's team brings to the matter in hand. The spirit of complementarity and exchange that characterizes a one-on-one mentoring relationship has also come to characterize these multi-dimensional partnerships.

In 2012 the Foundation took the step of establishing a prize specifically for outstanding mentors. Every two years the £25,000 Genesis Foundation Prize is awarded to someone whose work has demonstrably changed the practice and careers of emerging arts professionals. This is not some kind of feel-good, back-slapping exercise, much as the winners deserve recognition. They don't keep the prize money for themselves; instead they re-invest it in their mentoring activities. Once again, this is about the 'snowball' or 'domino' effect that mentoring can have.

One of my own mentors, when I was in my twenties, was Cardinal Basil Hume, who had been Archbishop of Westminster for a few years when I first met him. It

THE POWER OF TWO

was through him that I became involved in establishing
The Passage day centre for homeless people in Central
London. Every two weeks I would get together with him
for tea and we would discuss a diversity of topics, though
it was our shared concern for the homeless that was at
the heart of our mentoring relationship. Together, we
transformed that concern into action and The Passage
was the result. Cardinal Hume was more than 30 years
older than me and a very distinguished figure. It was
only natural that I would see him as my mentor, but,
when it came to the corporate disciplines of establishing
The Passage – the finances, fundraising, governance
and team-building – he was able to defer to me and my
training in business. For a young entrepreneur in the
field of giving, to have earned the respect and trust of
someone like Cardinal Hume was as motivating as it was
reassuring.

As you might expect, our shared faith was another of
our favourite themes. Cardinal Hume described the act
of Confession to a priest as 'an act of contrition when
one person admits their sins, anxieties and concerns to
another human being.' You could say that the impulse
and dynamic of Confession is echoed to some degree
in mentoring, which is similarly defined by a private
and sensitive discussion between two people. While
contrition – regret or remorse for something you have

done wrong – will obviously not feature in every mentoring conversation, as a mentee you are by definition confessing that you could do something better; you are showing humility by admitting that you have identified areas in which you could be stronger, and that you need help in taking yourself forward. At the same time, you are showing some healthy ambition. Humility and ambition make a surprisingly potent combination.

I was fortunate to find a transformative mentor in Cardinal Hume, and I do my utmost to continue to justify the belief he had in me. These days I frequently receive approaches from people who would be grateful for career advice or who are perhaps setting up a charity, and who hope that I could offer them some useful pointers. If I feel that they have thought about things carefully and that there might be something I could do for them, I will find a way of fitting a discussion with them into my schedule. I will make time for them.

None of us can ever know just what will transpire after a first meeting with someone new. Be that as it may, when I extend a welcome and an initial offer of support to someone who is, as yet, an unknown quantity, there is a message from the Bible that always comes to mind. It is found in the Book of Hebrews: 'Do not neglect to show hospitality to strangers, for thereby some have entertained angels unawares.' If your new encounter releases the Power of Two, it could prove transformational in ways you cannot predict. Whether mentoring or being mentored, by giving of yourself through your time and talent, you can open up more possibilities than you might ever have imagined.

12

Toughing it out

If you're looking for the easy option, entrepreneurial giving might not be for you. Entrepreneurs have a habit of questioning what they see in front of them: they tend not to favour the answers and choices that seem obvious or natural to everyone else. When it comes to an act of giving, it takes far more effort to take the entrepreneurial route, committing time and applying talent, than to settle for making a convenient financial transaction.

If your effort is consistently well-directed, it will produce results – if not immediately, over time. As an entrepreneur your job is to keep things moving forward, to retain a sense of purpose, always keeping the destination of your giving pilgrimage in mind. Inevitably, there will be times when you need to get tough – tough with yourself on a regular basis, and sometimes tough with people you are aiming to motivate, but tough every time when it comes to the aspects of life that you want to change.

In a similarly positive sense, there is an element of disruption in entrepreneurial giving. Even Benjamin Franklin, in his sociable, communicative, public-spirited way was a disruptor as he advocated action for the common good.

Disruption is often motivated by discomfort at what's going on in the world. But rather than sinking into doom and gloom, the entrepreneurial giver transforms that discomfort into healthy anger. Not anger in the sense of shouting at people and throwing things across the room, but anger in the sense of, 'Come on, guys, we really need to do something about this.'

There are some lines in St Paul's letter to the Ephesians that offer a lesson in handling anger and transforming it into a force for good: 'Be angry, and yet do not sin; do not let the sun go down on your anger … Let all bitterness and wrath and anger and clamour and slander be put away from you, along with all malice. Be kind to one another, tender-hearted, forgiving each other, just as God in Christ also has forgiven you.'

To put it another way, the only anger that can genuinely be described as healthy is anger that is channelled to compassionate, humane effect. It turns out that there is another T of entrepreneurial giving that comes into play here, and that is tenderness. People talk a lot about kindness and being kind, but this is something more. It is not just a 'good deed' that you do to or for someone, it is about a deeper, consistent, committed engagement.

The entrepreneur's healthy anger can also be filed under T if we call it temperament. Temperament is a form of passion – it fires you up and prompts you to take action. There are so many aspects of life on our big, complicated, strife-ridden planet that can justifiably trigger our anger. If we are to channel that anger productively, we need to pick our battles with care. Even the most energetic and optimistic entrepreneur can only commit to tackling a limited number of challenges at once.

First of all, you should focus on an issue that triggers a deep 'temperamental' response in you, but which at the same time feeds your instincts for compassion and tenderness. Emotion has a crucial role to play. Entrepreneurial giving is not done casually or with any sense of detachment. In fact, it should feel as if you have no alternative but to take action. At the same time you have no obligation to go along with the pack. If you find yourself putting your entrepreneurial energy into the same causes as the people around you, it should be because the motivation is coming from deep inside you. It's definitely not simply a matter of taking the option that is most readily available or at the top of the media agenda – unless, that is, you've spotted a particular niche that needs filling or you have a radical new solution to propose.

However fired up you get, it is worth heeding Mother Teresa's words about changing the world one person at a time. It pays to be realistic about what you can achieve with your time, talent and treasure at any particular moment. No matter how much talent you have, your time for giving is not unlimited and your access to treasure as an enabler cannot be taken as read. It is up to you to assess the nature and scale of the current challenge and to decide exactly where and how, with the talent and resources you have at your disposal, you stand to make a real difference.

As I've said before, the fundamental motivation for my giving comes from my belief in the primacy of human dignity. That's why I get angry when I see human dignity being compromised. It angers me when I think about the millions of people around the world who are enslaved through human trafficking. It angers me when I'm walking in London or New York and see that people are being left to sleep on the streets. It angers me when I hear that talented young people are not getting a chance to fulfil their creative potential because they're not privileged with access to the Bank of Mum and Dad.

There will be other injustices in the world that most strongly provoke anger in you, but you will know as well as I do that it is not enough simply to be angry. In fact, being angry doesn't do you any good, and in most cases – unless you have some serious traction – it doesn't do the

world any good either. As it says in the Epistle of James
in the Bible: 'Let every person be quick to hear, slow
to speak, slow to anger; for the anger of man does not
produce the righteousness of God.'

Rather than using up energy on experiencing and
expressing anger – and that includes 'activism' on
social media that basically amounts to sounding off
about your frustrations – you should use it to take
constructive action. You can sustain that action with
a sense of purpose, determination, tenacity and, when
needed, well-judged doses of temerity. On your giving
pilgrimage, your initial response to healthy anger might
be to make a donation to a relevant charity, but that
is only a first step in the right direction. If you are an
entrepreneur, anger will kickstart a durable and multi-
faceted process of transformation.

As I've also already said, I am by nature a 'glass-half-
full' person. If I feel angered by what I see, I don't just
let off steam or brood about it. My instinct is to come up
with ways of making things better, of applying my passion
to demonstrating compassion. Entrepreneurs tend to
be passionate about what they do, and it is passion that
helps them capture the interest and gain the trust of other
people. Passion will ignite your talents. Conversely, by
activating your talents thoughtfully and purposefully,
you can learn how to marshal and harness your passions
to still greater effect. You will find yourself diffusing less

energy and focusing your efforts more closely. This will further empower you in becoming an agent of change.

If you are going to make change happen, there are times when you do, indeed, need to get tough. When I say 'tough' here, I don't mean aggressive, overbearing or hard-boiled – remember, this is about compassion. What I mean is toughness that is rooted in honesty and integrity and in your desire, for everybody's sake, to obtain the best possible results. This toughness is grounded in a firm rationale and manifests in a confident strategy, but it doesn't entail obstinacy or inflexibility – that would be out of step with an entrepreneurial spirit. There is certainly an element of discipline involved – lining up the essentials so that your thinking and action have a robust backbone. It is the kind of toughness that goes with agility and an ability to roll with the punches and get back on your feet immediately. It is the toughness of resilience.

Some tough tactics – along with front-line tenacity – came into play when I was Chairman of Business Action on Homelessness. Part of our mission was to encourage homeless people to take an enterprising approach to finding work and so change the trajectory of their lives. For reasons I won't go into here, the homeless hostels would have let them stay in bed all day if they were lacking the motivation to get up. We sent people round to take them literally out of their comfort zone: to get them up and dressed and ready to go out and find employment. Along with the training and advice that Business Action on Homelessness supplied, this was another way of building their resilience.

Toughness is not just a matter of being able to stand your ground and achieve progress when faced with challenges. Sometimes, it is a matter of having to say 'no' to something that you don't feel is in line with your values, resources and objectives. This is not to say that the proposal at hand, if worthwhile, could not bear fruit in a different context.

At the Genesis Foundation we regularly find ourselves turning down ideas for interesting, imaginative and valid projects because they are not a match for our ethos and strategic criteria. Any proposal needs to be compatible with the Foundation's specific model for nurturing creative careers. Working closely with our partner organizations and their inspiring leaders, we have refined and honed it over the past 25 years. We continue to fill very closely defined gaps in the talent market. You could say that we need to be convinced that any proposal is – or, with some smart adaptation, could be – a match for Genesis's particular portfolio of talents. For everyone's sake, we want every project and programme we support to have the best possible chance of success. By this stage in the Foundation's existence we have a clear idea of the factors that will feed into success. This means we have now become tough enough to say 'no' with confidence and conviction (though politely and with sensitivity) because, with some trial and error along the way, we have learned exactly what it takes for us to be able to say 'yes'.

Once you have said 'yes' to collaboration with a person or a team – or if they have said 'yes' to you – any toughness you display towards them becomes an expression of the value you place on their talents. It stems from your belief in their potential to make a substantial contribution to your entrepreneurial project. If you are being 'tough' with them, it is because you respect what they have to offer and appreciate the way they can benefit your cause. Your aim is to maximize that benefit by making optimum use of their talents. You are challenging them as you challenge yourself, and it's often as we take on challenges – and find the toughness to rise to them – that we discover new talents in ourselves.

As we work at developing those talents, we are likely to need a dose of both temerity and tenacity. Temerity in the sense that we always run a risk when we test out a new approach, or when we try out a skill we have only recently consciously acquired. If things don't turn out exactly according to our expectations, we might find ourselves having to tough things out a little.

Hopefully, though, we won't have to engage in damage limitation. If we have been tough enough with ourselves along the way – applying rigour and our critical faculties to our planned actions, being humble enough to solicit and heed advice from mentors, and knowing when to be patient – any failure to progress or even any setbacks will be kept to a minimum.

Tenacity will come into play as we try and try again, having learned from any mistakes or failures – and that includes failures that are no fault of our own. I've already spoken about having to knock on 19 doors before the 20th door opens to you. That is one kind of tenacity. Another kind of tenacity is to keep working away at your giving projects, achieving what you can with the time and resources available, but also constantly learning, upping your game and developing and expanding your portfolio of talents.

At times, as both trial and error come into play, the going will get tough. Whenever it does, you will have an opportunity to build your resilience so that, in true entrepreneurial style, you can bounce back stronger, ready to rise to the next challenge. Sometimes you will make a big leap forward, but mostly you will find yourself taking things step by step. If you're ready to think in terms of changing the world one person at a time, that is more than enough.

Let's leave the last word on tenacity in giving to St Paul in his Epistle to the Galatians: 'Each one should test their own actions. Then they can take pride in themselves alone, without comparing themselves to someone else, for each one should carry their own load ... Let us not become weary in doing good, for at the proper time we will reap a harvest if we do not give up. Therefore, as we have opportunity, let us do good to all people ...'

13

The ties that bind

You can't do it all alone. That's as true of giving as of any other form of endeavour – and it's especially true of entrepreneurial giving. Every entrepreneur needs to possess (or unearth) a talent for establishing and cultivating ties with a diversity of people. I've learned that in my business life, and I've learned it through my activity with charities and NGOs since I was a teenager.

Each one of us, no matter what our age, occupation or interests, has the potential to become an agent for change. One of the major routes to achieving change runs through our personal and professional networks – or, expressed as Ts of entrepreneurial giving, our ties, our teams and our tribes. Networks have always existed in the physical world. For me at least, it will always be the 'real life' networks that matter most, but there is no denying the power of online networks in our society today.

If you have an entrepreneurial spirit, you are always ready to expand your networks – putting yourself out there (in person and online) with a sense of purpose … keeping an open mind, never quite knowing what you might discover, talking to new people and looking to build new relationships. It's never a case of 'Been there, done that,' or 'I can just go it alone.'

You have to keep listening, learning, connecting and finding common ground and a common purpose. Any tensions you encounter along the way can shed new light on your way of thinking and how best to handle any differences of opinion: as an entrepreneur, you can derive valuable insight from every experience. Nothing is wasted.

Some of your new relationships will lead to collaboration in the short or medium term and some of them will lead to trusted partnerships. Some, of course, will lead nowhere at all – but that's the way things go. To a certain degree it's a numbers game, but it's not a game of random numbers: instinct and judgement play a major role in building networks that hold value.

It pays to be selective and to start off with what sales professionals call qualified leads. In other words you have profiled the people you meet as being 'more likely to buy'. However quickly your networks grow, or however extensive they become, you should continue to welcome new people into them. A network that falls into stasis soon starts to lose its energy and electricity. Equally, if you keep yourself moving, there are always new networks to be explored.

When you hear someone described as 'well connected' or 'well networked', it usually suggests a person who knows a lot of influential or 'useful' people. But in a fair-minded, honest relationship, being useful works both ways. A well-networked person has to be ready to be useful too, ready to share their time, talent and ties (in other words their contacts) with people who are valued and trusted enough to belong in their network. Responsibilities come with being well networked. It is a matter of give as well as take.

In my day job I've worked with many clients who have entrepreneurship in their background, but my own professional life has been principally anchored in national and international organizations of some size. They have been firmly structured and peopled by legions of specialists organized into teams. Obviously, as a member of a team or as a manager of teams, success lies in sharing a clear purpose with a strong line-up of people. Those people should complement you in their talents and expertise, they should complement each other, and they should know how to make best use of their professional time. The way St Paul put it in his letter to the Romans was 'We have different gifts, according to the grace given to each of us.'

A team becomes most powerful when the people within it feed off each other, benefiting from each other's knowledge, insights and ideas as they collaborate. It means so much to be able to trust the people in the teams around you, to know you can leave them to get on with their work – in other words, you can rely on them.

But if you have an entrepreneurial spirit, you never simply take the people in those teams as they are – and you certainly never take them for granted. An entrepreneur doesn't stand still and is always looking for more.

You keep your feelers out and you keep finding out just what motivates those people, what makes them tick. You might find yourself nurturing their talents, even sometimes acting as a formal or informal mentor. You will also keep track in your organization of people in teams beyond your own – there is always talent-spotting (and talent-unearthing) that can be done. And if you have the kind of job that faces outwards from your organization, you will constantly be finding people you can integrate into your network. And if you hear about people you feel you ought to know, you will find a way of getting to know them.

All these principles, which give rise to a constant process of discovery, can be applied in your practice of entrepreneurial giving, as you join, assemble or tap into teams, and as you build support for your purpose and projects. To quote from another of St Paul's letters, found in the Book of Hebrews, 'And let us consider how to stir up one another to love and good works.'

If the declared mission of the Genesis Foundation is to nurture the careers and build the resilience of outstanding creative professionals, in business parlance it is about investment in human capital through the development and reinforcement of talent. In a more concrete, less philosophical sense it represents an investment in the UK's vibrant and globally admired creative economy.

In a creative career, as in any other kind of career, networks are important. They are especially important for the substantial proportion of creative professionals who are self-employed. In a sector like the performing arts or film and TV – so often a 'gig economy' where expert freelance skills can be required at a moment's notice – it makes all the difference to know someone who knows someone. Equally, it is good to be the someone that someone knows.

The Genesis Foundation, which puts its belief in training, mentoring and networks, reflects and fosters this culture. At the same time it reinforces the resilience of talented people whose livelihoods rely on it. Networks – whether new or established, structured or informal – are a recurring theme in the Genesis programmes run by a variety of respected and dynamic cultural institutions. It is those institutions that form the core of the Genesis Foundation's extensive and diverse professional network, though the Foundation itself is run by a very compact, highly focused team.

I always insist that, when it comes to networking, nothing beats face-to-face, in-the-flesh contact. That being said, there is absolutely no doubt that online networking now plays a crucial role in virtually any kind of career development: there's a reason why LinkedIn can claim one billion members worldwide.

In 2004, the year after LinkedIn came on the scene, London's innovative Young Vic Theatre, conceived in the early 1970s as 'a new kind of theatre for a new generation', launched the online Genesis Network. A community platform for directors and other backstage professionals, the Network became one of the first dedicated online spaces for UK theatre-makers looking to make new contacts, find new collaborators, colleagues and projects, and identify work opportunities. Over its 20-year existence, membership of the Network – which covered the whole country and was free to use – grew from 200 to 2,500. When the pandemic brought the live performing arts to a standstill, the Young Vic team provided online workshops as a lifeline to the Network's members, but at any time the Network's greatest strength lay in the way its members supported and mentored each other.

They built each other's knowledge and skills and flagged up projects and jobs they heard about. When the going got tough they were there to help and offer encouragement. The Genesis Network showed that technology, when put to thoughtful and purposeful use, can very much stand as one of the Ts of entrepreneurial giving, here integrating talent, time, trust, 'two' (one-on one mentoring) and ties.

There was another T in there too: transmission, in other words the passing-on and exchange of principles and ideas. Both online and in real life, the Network's members demonstrated generosity and respect to each other. As passionate people, full of ideas and eager to succeed, they could so easily have found themselves being competitive or combative in their stance. Instead, as active members of a network that nurtured a sense of common ground and a collaborative spirit, they were mutually supportive: they shared ideas, leads and best practice, helping each other to survive and make progress in a challenging environment.

In choosing to belong to an open-hearted, purposeful and confident community, the members of the Genesis Network were not only affirming each other's worth as professionals, they were affirming each other's human dignity. They might not have thought of it in those specific terms – 'dignity' is a word that tends to be associated with an older demographic – but that is absolutely what they were doing.

Life as a theatre-maker, especially as a freelancer, is often unpredictable – it is bound to have its downs as well as its ups – but people like the members of the Genesis

Network exercise their freedom by choosing to work in a profession they love. Freedom of choice is a pillar of human dignity.

Sadly, among the most profound challenges to human dignity in the world today are the scourges of modern slavery and human trafficking. Slaves, often deprived of their freedom through conflict and disruption, are used to satisfy the demand for cheap labour in a globalized market. It is estimated that 50 million people around the world are enslaved, that some 28 million people are in forced labour, and that one in four victims of modern slavery are children. Human trafficking and modern slavery are global businesses that operate mercilessly through complex criminal networks – there could well be some modern slavery going on, well under the radar, in your neighbourhood.

It takes robust humanitarian networks to work against those criminal networks. That is why I co-founded the Arise Foundation in 2015 and went on to chair it for five years. Arise embodies its stated values of respect for human dignity, humility and trust by building and consolidating networks that empower people working at key locations around the world to combat human trafficking, on the frontline and on the ground.

The idea for the organization grew from my advisory and fundraising involvement, at the suggestion of the late Pope Francis, with the anti-trafficking work of communities of religious sisters around the world. Just as some religious sisters run schools and hospitals, others devote their energies to the sometimes dangerous work of suppressing the modern slave trade and to rescuing its victims and supporting its survivors. These religious communities now constitute just one of the specialist front-line groups whose work is furthered by the Arise Foundation through advocacy, training and networks, right there in the places and communities where ordinary people – women, children and men – could be at risk of enslavement.

In their very different ways, the Genesis Network at the Young Vic and those communities of religious sisters can be seen as membership organizations. The concept of a membership organization is well established in the broader environment of giving and charities.

If someone joins a closely knit group as a member, rather than acting at arm's length as a donor or as an external volunteer, they feel a greater sense of commitment and ownership. In addition, they are aware of a greater responsibility to their fellow members and the organization as a whole. They are part of a living organism as they join other members of the group on a mission – and on a giving pilgrimage. It becomes only natural that they should get out there and network on behalf of their organization, playing a role in awareness-raising, outreach and potentially fundraising too.

If you are planning to launch a charitable organization of some kind, it is worth thinking of it as a membership organization. This does not necessarily involve a financial donation from the word go: money is, of course, always welcome for a charity, but a firm commitment of time or talent stands to create a closer initial bond and a deeper long-term relationship. If a supporter's commitment runs simply to making a donation rather than direct and active involvement, it risks becoming a box-ticking exercise: 'Job done for the moment. I'll leave it to the charity to remind me when it's time for the next donation.'

Going deeper, you will stand to get the best out of any potential supporter or donor if you genuinely make them feel they could have a durable place in your organization – that their time, talents and personal qualities will be valued now and in the future. That means so much more than just being seen as a source of money. We all know that a strong sense of belonging can do a great deal for our self-esteem and, ultimately, our human dignity. Its significance should in no way be underestimated.

When you form a new organization, you create a new working community that needs embedding in its environment of existing communities – geographical, professional and social. You also need to think carefully about its relationship with the community you are intending to serve: how will you, with your specific capabilities and resources, do the best for the people you want to help (your beneficiaries), and how comfortable will they feel with the approach you are taking?

There are no more important stakeholders than the beneficiaries. If your feelings about an issue are strong enough to motivate you to establish a group or charity to address it, your call to action might well have been a direct, even life-changing experience of that issue. On the other hand, there is no reason why your experience should take a standard form or come from a predictable direction.

For instance, a few years ago I became involved with creating a coaching academy for the Riding for the Disabled Association, which has a presence in more than 470 locations around the UK – quite a network.

Several times, people pointed out to me that I am not what you'd call a signed-up member of the equestrian community. When it comes to riding, I'm far more likely to be seen on a bike than a horse. When I was introduced to the Riding for the Disabled Association, what inspired me to take things further was the opportunity to put a mentoring model into action. The association nurtures the talents and refines the skills of specialist riding coaches – these are the people who work hands-on and face-to-face with disabled riders. The academy and its mentoring equip the coaches to provide the riders with a deeply therapeutic, life-enhancing, maybe transformative experience that is emblematic of their human dignity. I really don't have to be a horseman myself to appreciate how much that matters.

Riding for the Disabled draws its energy and operational strength from an abundance of local groups, mostly run by volunteers, in England, Scotland, Wales and Northern Ireland. By contrast, The Passage, though a UK leader in the field of homelessness, is closely identified with a single location, Carlisle Place near Victoria Station in London. It has been headquartered there since 1980, when I helped to establish it as a volunteer, and it is now very much part of the scenery and the community in Westminster.

It no doubt helps that Carlisle Place has been associated with care for people in need since the mid-nineteenth century, when it became home to the Convent of the Daughters of Charity of St Vincent de Paul. This living tradition further empowers The Passage as it engages in outreach and consolidates and extends its network. Whenever we embark on fundraising for The Passage, it is heartening and reassuring to receive support from the City of Westminster, which fully appreciates the importance of the service The Passage supplies to Westminster's population, and from local residents and businesses, who see it as part of the ecosystem. There is a sense of everyone being in it together.

From my personal point of view, The Passage has been part of my life for 40 years and I have felt privileged to evolve with it, assuming a variety of formal responsibilities along the way. What remains at the heart of the relationship are those regular occasions when I go in and help out at the day centre, spending time with some of the homeless people there or just getting on with practical tasks, like cleaning, tidying or serving food. You could say that the people at The Passage, a multi-faceted community at the intersection of a multitude of networks, have become like family for me – and ties don't come any closer than that.

14

Tears of gratitude

If you want to be good at giving, you have to be ready to be good at receiving. You can only give in the truest sense – with your heart and your soul, in the cause of the common good – if you learn to strike a healthy balance between what it means to give and what it means to receive.

That balance is fundamental to our existence. As human beings we live in a series of concentric communities: our personal community, our local community, our national community and, encompassing them all, a global community. To varying degrees the members of all those communities are dependent on each other.

In 1995, Pope John Paul II wrote: 'God has entrusted the life of every individual to his or her fellow human beings, brothers and sisters, according to the law of reciprocity in giving and receiving.' What he was saying was that each one of us carries a huge responsibility for the people around us. Through giving to other people, you are shouldering that responsibility. But in return, according to the law of reciprocity, there are billions of people who have some kind of responsibility to you. Each one of us relies on so many people in so many ways – practical, emotional and spiritual – for our existence and our well-being. They deserve our gratitude for what they do for us.

Pope John Paul II always emphasized the importance of recognizing the gifts we receive, whether they are gifts from other people or gifts from God. In acknowledging a gift you are above all nurturing a spirit of appreciation. But, in being grateful, you are also fostering humility. By not in any way taking gifts for granted, by not seeing them as 'owing' to you or as a way to bolster your ego, you are also succeeding in being humble. At the same time you are affirming the significance of a relationship that draws strength from both giving and receiving. When we do justice to other people, we are also doing justice to God.

A gift can take a multitude of forms and one of those forms is help. Sometimes we have to remind ourselves that it is not a sign of weakness to accept help when it is offered to us. Help, if it is needed, is something you should welcome both gratefully and graciously. There is more at stake here than your personal benefit. When you willingly accept help, you celebrate your status – maybe even your privileged position – as a member of the human community. The world can only thrive if we are genuinely ready to work to make life better for each other.

Though I am speaking from the heart (and soul) here, there is a certain irony in all this. The thing is, though I hope I've been pretty good at giving since I was maybe six or seven years old, I haven't always been very good at receiving. It's a skill – or maybe a blessing – that I have had to acquire over the years.

When I was a teenager I was awarded a prize by my school in Massachusetts for the work I had done on Operation Venus, the helpline I mentioned earlier, which answered young people's questions about sexually transmitted diseases. The award was a total surprise to me. When my name was announced, I was so taken aback – even shocked – by the honour that tears came to my eyes. But those tears were also prompted by a striking realization. In one of the light bulb moments of my life, it dawned on me that I was being thanked for something I hadn't seen as 'giving'. As far as I had been concerned, it was simply something I had to do.

When I got Operation Venus going, it was because I wanted to find a solution to what I saw as an important problem. Of course, I could see there would be a benefit for society – the common good, again – but I didn't see myself as some kind of budding benefactor. I was just getting on with the job. There was no alternative if we were going to try and get things fixed. Maybe one of the defining features of an entrepreneur is simply perceiving a necessity to 'do it yourself'. You see no other choice but to get your hands dirty, involving yourself at grass-roots level.

Receiving that award as a 16-year-old, and starting to learn how to receive gratitude, was a formative experience for me. I had another lesson in gratitude about ten years later, when I had moved to London. It was very different, and it didn't involve any tears, but it was equally memorable.

It happened in the early days of my involvement with The Passage and its work with people experiencing homelessness. It must have been something like 2 a.m. on a dank, wintry night and I was out on Victoria Street keeping an eye out for people sleeping rough. McDonald's was open late and I ended up buying burgers, coffees and apple pies for eight or so homeless men who clearly needed a hot meal. I handed them out the food. Some of them said 'Thank you'. Some of them didn't – but that didn't bother me: you never know how people are going to respond in that kind of situation, and I was doing it for their sake, not mine. Still, they all seemed pleased to have the food ... apart from one guy. When I gave him his apple pie, he handed it back and said, 'I'd prefer cherry.'

I was so nonplussed by this that my instinctive reaction was to laugh. Part of me wanted to say, 'Hey, I bought you dinner ... You should be grateful. Why don't you like my apple pie?' Then I remembered that he was the one who mattered here, not me. He was acknowledging my gift, but he was also taking the opportunity to assert his human dignity, making clear to me that he still had a choice. It absolutely wasn't a case – to coin a defeatist phrase – of 'beggars can't be choosers'. Frankly, it was up to me to be grateful that he felt comfortable enough in the situation to say what was on his mind.

The phrase that I needed to coin for myself that night on Victoria Street comes from the Bible, when St Paul cites the words of Jesus: 'It is more blessed to give than to receive.' Maybe I had forgotten what a fortunate position I was in. It was a privilege to be able to provide some tasty hot food for eight cold, hungry men who didn't have a roof over their head. When it came down to it, that was reward enough. There was already plenty for me to be grateful for.

In St Luke's Gospel there is another, longer quote from Jesus which, for me, puts this whole story of giving, receiving and cherry pie in context. Here, Jesus is talking to a prosperous man in his home: 'When you give a luncheon or dinner, do not invite your friends, your brothers or sisters, your relatives, or your rich neighbours; if you do, they may invite you back and so you will be repaid. But when you give a banquet, invite the poor, the crippled, the lame, the blind, and you will be blessed. Although they cannot repay you, you will be repaid at the resurrection of the righteous.'

In the course of my personal giving pilgrimage I've encountered some amazing people. One of them was literally a saint – Mother Teresa, who died in 1997 at the age of 87. She was tireless and relentlessly determined in her work for the poor and the sick. Though she is most closely associated with Calcutta, she was a figure of international influence. In New York she established hospices for people suffering from AIDS, which at the time could not be treated. It was there that I worked with her on fundraising to buy buildings to turn into hospices. She seemed to be able to perform miracles for any cause she believed in and we met our financial targets with astonishing speed. Mother Teresa was a woman of great strength, but also of great humility. She saw herself as a servant of God and never sought praise or recognition for what she did. One day I asked her about this and she said, 'It is enough thanks for me to see people comforted, sleeping peacefully or dying with dignity.'

Amazing in a different way from Mother Teresa was Cardinal Basil Hume – who, as I've already said, became a mentor to me. In 2001, two years after his death, he came very much to mind when I learned that Pope John Paul II had made me a Knight of St Gregory the Great in recognition of work I had done with the homeless. Once again, this was an award that came as a total surprise, and once again the news brought tears to my eyes. I didn't know what to think – as I've said,

I haven't always been very good at receiving. 'What would Cardinal Hume's view have been?' I wondered. He would have said, 'Accept the award in the spirit in which it was given. You'll be setting an example to the entire giving community.' In other words, it would have a multiplier effect. And in a world governed by the law of reciprocity in giving and receiving, that has as many positive implications for people doing the giving as for people who are receiving. We find ourselves in a win-win situation for the common good.

Having mentioned John Paul II a number of times in this chapter, I'll leave the final words on giving and receiving to him. His statement could hardly be clearer, more conclusive or more resonant: 'The meaning of life is found in giving and receiving love.'

15

The tech tempest

Can you remember life before the Internet? I'll freely admit that I can. There's no way I can call myself a digital native. In fact, I started my giving pilgrimage more than 30 years before we all began going online in our everyday lives. Inevitably my experience of the pre-digital world, and everything I learned in that world, influences my views on the role that technology has to play in the whole culture of giving, today and tomorrow.

Technology continues to transform almost every aspect of our existence. It really has become hard to know how we would survive without it. (Though sometimes it's worth considering how you'd respond to a situation if you didn't have the latest technology to hand … It's an exercise that can help you become more resourceful and creative in your thinking.) Not only does technology develop with astonishing speed, we adopt it and adapt to it with astonishing speed. An app or a gadget that seems life-changing when we first use it soon gets taken for granted. Before long we become ready to move on to the next shiny 'must-have' innovation that the tech companies dream up and feed to us.

Just think how technology has transformed the fundamental giving task of fundraising. In a short time we've progressed far beyond the once-standard basic solution, which was to stand on a busy street corner and rattle coins in a collecting tin. (How often do you even handle a coin these days?) Now, anyone can conceive and launch a fundraising campaign, whether small-scale or ambitious, in a matter of minutes. You just tap into ready-made digital platforms, where you can set up the campaign, run it and then track the results in real time.

Crowdfunding has become so much part of the scenery that we hardly think about the 'crowd' component any more. All the same, crowdfunding provides a graphic demonstration of the Internet's power to instantly alert large numbers of people and prompt them into action. Within moments you can assemble and activate your fundraising tribe. Crowdfunding really does go to show that 'every little helps'. Beyond these standard mechanics of fundraising, entire relationships in giving are now established and developed online.

When it comes to entrepreneurial giving, in comparison to the days before the Internet and social media, it takes a lot less time and effort to research, build networks, and seek out potential mentors. Gaining initial access to the kind of people you need has become much easier.

But that doesn't automatically mean that it has become easier to achieve the results you want. In the online environment there is huge competition for attention. Everyone is bombarded with information and approaches. You still need to find ways of making yourself stand out, of getting the right people to take notice of you and take you seriously as someone with a clear vision and a credible mission. This is where you need to find powerful ways of giving expression to your talents and demonstrating their value. Temerity and tenacity will also have a role to play in getting through to people and going on to establish genuine, durable ties, build functioning teams, and nurture and sustain trust.

And while we are on the Ts of entrepreneurial giving, temperament has a place in this discussion too. If temperament is the anger you feel at what's wrong with the world, you might well want to express that anger on social media. You probably think of that as activism. But expressing your anger should not become an end in itself. That can happen all too easily on social media, where an indignant statement can lead to a destructive confrontation in a matter of moments – more quickly than in a face-to-face discussion.

If you believe in entrepreneurial giving, you have to make something of that anger by channelling it into purposeful, constructive action. If you have built up support online, now is the time to transform it into support in the real world. If you can rely on a constituency of people who feel the same way you do and agree with the arguments you put forward, you have the foundations of a venture that will achieve something for the common good.

Essentially, what I am saying here is, don't let life mediated through technology become a substitute for real, in-the-flesh life. Technology is a fantastic facilitator, but you must never forget that you are the one in charge – the thinking, feeling human being who is driving your giving project. And what you can bring to every eventuality and interaction is your individual, entrepreneurial, compassionate human touch. Technology, even the most cutting-edge AI app, just can't do that. The human touch matters in any context or environment, but it matters most when you are in the room with someone, talking, listening and sensing.

We all know that artificial intelligence is rapidly getting better at absorbing, classifying and simulating human thinking and responses. What matters in entrepreneurial giving are your distinctive (and instinctive) talents and your personal, maybe idiosyncratic thoughts and responses. No other human being is exactly like you and you are the person (not the digital entity) in charge.

Idiosyncrasies can have their uses, making you more striking and memorable and pointing the way to different, maybe innovative answers. The possibilities of AI are, of course, huge. No doubt we will soon be able to draw on the wisdom of AI 'mentors', and in the years to come, entrepreneurs of every kind will be raising their game with selective, savvy and insightful use of AI. In due course, AI might come to replace some of your skills, but digital code and algorithms will never replace the God-given talents and passions that you, and only you possess. If are really going to achieve results as an entrepreneur in giving, nothing beats your human touch.

16

Taking a trial run

If at first you don't succeed, try, try again. How many times have you heard people say that? If you're going to make a success of entrepreneurial giving, you're not going to give up easily. It takes some dedication and it takes some tenacity – which, after all, is one of the Ts I've talked about. But there's another T, only mentioned in passing up till now, that can help you find success, and that's trial. There is a place in entrepreneurial giving for testing out ideas and initiatives.

No matter how enthusiastic, talented and knowledgeable you are, no matter how much homework you've done or how carefully you've calculated your risks, there is no guarantee you are going to get things right first time. Circumstances and events (and, let's face it, possibly a mistake or two) might dictate otherwise. There is no shame in admitting to yourself that your success is not guaranteed. There is no shame in admitting it to other people either, as long as you can also provide evidence of responsible and constructive thinking.

You can supply that evidence if you systematically build trials into your practice of giving. With the help of a trial, you increase your chances of getting things right. It might require some patience, but it will be worth it: by strategically exercising some initial caution, you will be able to act with greater confidence further down the line.

This is why manufacturers test-market their products, why tech companies release beta software, why designers and engineers build prototypes, why retailers and restaurants stage 'soft openings', and why there are dress rehearsals and preview nights in show business. A trial involves a degree of exposure, so you still have to make every effort to do things as well as you can, but by limiting your exposure you gain a greater degree of control. If you handle the trial wisely and methodically, people will make allowances for anything that doesn't go quite to plan. At best, they will feel they are contributing to a process that will enhance your chances of success, both in the trial and in your future endeavours.

You might have big ambitions for your giving – if so, that is very much to your credit – but that doesn't mean you should reject the idea of taking comparatively small steps, certainly in the initial stages of your giving pilgrimage. In fact, by taking things cautiously in the early stages, you could substantially increase your chances of sustainable success in the longer term.

A constructive and low-risk way to make a start in entrepreneurial giving is by volunteering for an organization you admire and whose values and goals you share. No matter how big the ideas you have, you shouldn't reject an opportunity to volunteer in even a minor capacity.

First of all, you will be making a contribution to the organization's endeavours, but as you do so you will be gaining an understanding of your 'market'. With your entrepreneurial eye you will also be considering how you could make a more substantial contribution to the cause, whether as a resource for an existing organization or by going it alone. As a volunteer you will observe practices you want to emulate, but maybe also practices that need improvement or rethinking. You might well identify some future entrepreneurial opportunities in the form of a gap or niche that you believe you can fill, or an alternative route or solution that you can propose.

Volunteering really can lead to bigger things. When I first came to London from the USA in the early 1980s, I volunteered with a small charity that was providing basic food and day care for homeless people. Today, as I've said elsewhere, I still volunteer for The Passage, which has grown into a substantial, multi-dimensional, professionally run organization. Now, as a leader in the homelessness sector, it provides a range of services to a far greater number of people than it did over 40 years ago. It means a lot to me to have been a member of the small team of people who identified the potential for The Passage to expand its ambitions and its remit, and who went on to play a determining role in its evolution.

Once you've tried volunteering in various capacities, maybe taking on some formal roles on the frontline or in management, you might consider it time to launch your own, distinctive project in the field of giving. In the first instance, I would recommend keeping your project on a modest or even a miniature scale. Start off with a smartly conceived pilot project rather than a full-blown launch. Keep your activities tightly targeted and don't be tempted to let your ambitions run away with you. Be realistic about the resources you have (and that includes your own time) and about what you are aiming to achieve. Once again, we go back to Mother Teresa's belief in the value and wisdom of changing the world one person at a time.

Set yourself a realistic objective, and define your project clearly with a fixed duration and with a distinct beginning, middle and an end. Mark out its scope by thinking about how many people you want (and need) to get actively involved as stakeholders, and about how many lives the project might stand to change in some way. Those changes could be a matter of a tangible or physical improvement or they could be a matter of altering people's thinking. Once you have succeeded in getting your project underway, and as obstacles or opportunities arise, you are almost certain to need to make some adjustments to your plan and resources. This is all part of the entrepreneurial experience and all part of the constant learning process that goes with it.

When you have completed your pilot project, make an assessment of how well it went and how well it performed against your expectations and the objectives you set. Ask the opinions of the other people involved – and that should include the people who stood to benefit from the pilot project: they are key stakeholders.

Be ready to listen carefully to whatever they say. We all like to hear praise, but we should also be ready to take note of justifiable criticism. How you assess and respond to that criticism is, of course, up to you, but it is better not to dismiss it out of hand. Optimism and enthusiasm are part of being an entrepreneur, but so is having a clear eye, a cool head and a streak of humility. Humility is a great help when it comes to keeping whatever you are doing in proportion.

If, having completed your pilot project, you decide to keep your entrepreneurial activities on a modest level rather than scaling up, that is in no way an admission of failure. As long as you are achieving positive results for your chosen cause and not putting excessive strain on your resources, then you are winning. If, for any reason, the pilot project doesn't work out the way you would have hoped, any negative implications will be limited. Vitally, as with any entrepreneurial endeavour, you will have learned from the experience of the trial. With the help of the insights you have acquired, you can either adjust your model next time, or branch out and try something different.

I can confidently say I am speaking from experience here. In the very early days of the Genesis Foundation we undertook an ambitious, high-profile project with a prestigious institutional partner. Exciting in itself, the project was not the best match for the particular talents that Genesis had to offer at the time. It gave us the opportunity to nurture the careers of emerging artists, but, beyond that basic match, we had not defined it with sufficient rigour against strategic or practical criteria.

We commissioned three musical works from young composers. They were received with radically varying degrees of enthusiasm – and some of the critics' judgements were pretty bruising. By running before we knew just how we wanted to walk, and by arousing such high expectations with the project partnership, we had exposed emerging creative artists to the harshest of spotlights.

One of the Foundation's greatest strengths now lies in the partners we choose to work with, but, for a number of reasons, that early partnership failed to jell. It wasn't a happy experience, but we learned a great deal from it. In a sense, though this wasn't our explicit intention, it acted as a pilot project. By the time it was over, we had a much firmer idea of exactly where the Genesis Foundation should head and of the conditions we needed to set for any future partnership.

Since then, an important component of our Genesis partnerships – which now run for a minimum of two years – is a constant process of mutual consultation, of identifying gaps, possible improvements and opportunities. Like us, our partners understand that there is an iterative aspect to any working relationship or living project.

However firmly your projects are conceived and mapped out, and however well they are going, they will always embrace an element of trial. If you handle your planning with insight and skill, there will only be a minimum of proverbial error to go with it. As you make your way on your giving pilgrimage, a trial can serve to keep you firmly on track and sure of your path.

17

Building a generous society

In thinking about *A Talent for Giving* I've thought a lot about the Parable of the Talents, those three servants and what they do with the money entrusted to them by their boss. 'Then he who had received the five talents went and traded with them, and made another five talents. And likewise he who had received two gained two more also. But he who had received one went and dug in the ground, and hid his lord's money.'

As I've said several times, I'm a glass-half-full person – and for me there's a glass-half-full way of looking at the third servant, the one-talent man. In the parable, he is seen to fail – and, sadly, he is punished for failing. From my point of view, he cannot be defined simply by his lack of achievement. Nor should we unthinkingly condone his punishment. Instead, we should take a generous stance by looking for more in him: we should take the opportunity to identify his potential for growth. For all we know – and for all he knows – he could have a five-talent man somewhere in him, though he might more realistically aspire to two-talent or maybe three-talent level. Whatever the case, he needs to take a lesson from the harsh experience described in the parable. How can he transcend his current limitations and release any potential he might hold – for his own sake and possibly for the common good too?

It doesn't look as though he is going to get any help from his boss or from his two fellow servants. If we were on the spot, we could offer him some compassion, a listening ear, encouragement and ideas, and perhaps a little mentoring. We could take him through the events of the parable and suggest how he might have done things differently. But as things stand, it is up to him to pick himself up, dust himself off and set about unearthing his metaphorical talents. He will be working on himself and he will be working by himself. Whether he can find the resources and resilience to do this, we will never know.

The parable is, of course, 'just a story', but through their symbolic narratives, parables provide us with guidance and learning that we can apply to our own lives.

First and foremost, as I look afresh at the Parable of the Talents, I am struck by the way we all have something of one-talent man in us. We can be too ready to accept what we believe to be our limitations. There are latent talents lying deep within each of us, but we need to have courage and commitment to unearth them. If we succeed in finding that courage and commitment, we are already showing entrepreneurial spirit.

The outcome of the parable also reminds me that, when it comes to unearthing our talent for giving, the ultimate responsibility lies with each of us as an individual. No one else can look as deep inside us as we can ourselves. Yes, other people can provide insights and point us in the right direction, and maybe they can help us to develop and apply a talent we've already identified, but in the end the only person who can really unearth your talents is you.

When you think of an entrepreneur, you generally think of a person of action – someone energetic and energizing who excels at identifying opportunities and seizing them. But entrepreneurial giving is not all about action, at least not all the time.

When it comes to unearthing your talents, you need to take the opportunity for some quiet but probing introspection. The time for introspection is not just at the beginning of your giving pilgrimage, when you first set about unearthing your talents. It also comes when you choose to make a pause as you progress along your pilgrimage route and learn from your experiences. This is not the kind of introspection that cuts you off from the world as you simply lose yourself in your thoughts: it has a purpose. Entrepreneurial giving is driven by deep-seated emotion and conviction, but through some calm, methodical analysis you will gain a deeper understanding of what you have to offer. By regularly making a careful assessment of yourself, you will build the kind of self-awareness that will keep you and your giving heading firmly in the right direction.

I said right at the beginning of this book that giving is all about you, and it is through systematic introspection that you define and redefine yourself. It will help you keep pace with your passions and talents as they emerge and evolve. Not only will you gain new clarity on your current activities, you will line yourself up for your next challenge or new project.

As you follow a path of entrepreneurial giving, times and circumstances will change. You will enjoy some successes and possibly suffer some failures too. As you absorb all this and respond to it, it is only natural (and healthy) to want to recalibrate and reset from time to time. Your environment is not static, and neither are you or your talents, but however things shift around you and inside you, you can draw strength and confidence from your essential beliefs. They can always serve as your point of reference.

It could also help you to remember that, whatever happens, you have God on your side. The Book of Joshua sums this up: 'Be strong and courageous. Do not be frightened, and do not be dismayed, for the Lord your God is with you wherever you go.'

Another constant for me has been my belief in human dignity. Not that I would have expressed my belief in those terms as a child in the 1960s, when I set out on my giving pilgrimage from what we then called a soup kitchen. The world has changed hugely since then – and I, of course, have changed too in some respects. But, as I've made my way, I've never lost that fundamental glass-half-full attitude and I've never lost my passion for contributing to the common good by learning to change the world one person at a time.

I hope I will always keep an open mind and remain receptive to new ideas, opportunities and approaches. I hope too that I will remain resourceful when it comes to finding my way to solutions. The world's age-old problems still need to be solved. Some of them may never be solved, but we should never be discouraged from doing what we can to alleviate them. Even if we change things for the better for just one person on one stage of our pilgrimage, we are succeeding in our giving.

Meanwhile, new problems continue to arise as the world moves on, posing new challenges for all of us. You could say that an entrepreneur's work is never done – maybe because entrepreneurial giving becomes enmeshed with your life. It is not the kind of work you can just do when it comes to mind or when someone reminds you about it with a request for money or help. It is more like an integral part of your being. Over the course of your life, you should hope to drive maybe four, five or six substantial, sustainable projects that have grown directly from your passions, beliefs and talents.

Of all the many charitable organizations I've been closely involved with over the years – from Human Rights Watch to the J. Paul Getty Trust, from the American Associates of the Saint Catherine Foundation to Business Action on Homelessness in the UK – I've been in at absolute grass-roots level with Operation Venus (the STD helpline, when I was a teenager), with The Passage day centre for the homeless when I was in my twenties and thirties, with the Genesis Foundation and Benjamin Franklin House in my forties, and with Arise, which combats human trafficking, in my fifties. I turn 70 in 2026 and there could be more to come! I find entrepreneurial giving as motivating, illuminating and invigorating as I ever did. I need it in my life. The pilgrimage continues.

Another reason it continues is that entrepreneurial giving is not about undertaking one significant endeavour that either succeeds or fails. It is not a matter of start and stop and that's it, of ticking entrepreneurial giving off your to-do list. Your deep-seated talents don't fade and your driving passions don't subside. An entrepreneur is constantly learning and developing, always ready to re-examine the processes that feed into giving, always ready to refine and hone the disciplines that translate positive thinking into productive action. As an entrepreneur, you will commit to being rigorous and diligent as you look for different, more effective ways of promoting the common good through your particular set of talents. You might do this alone, but you are more likely to do it in partnership with people who are like-minded and who inspire trust in you, whose talents complement yours and so enhance and reinforce your capacities for doing good.

When you embark on your first giving endeavour, you might want to take things carefully. There is a lot to be said for exercising a little strategic caution, as long as you always retain your enthusiasm, your forward momentum and your clear sense of purpose. An entrepreneur is always ready to take the initiative, but a canny entrepreneur also remains ready to take advice from people they trust and to test the waters before diving in completely. Once you have gained some initial experience of entrepreneurial giving, you can look forward to accumulating insights and to bringing greater assurance to every subsequent endeavour.

By the time you've been through the whole giving exercise once or twice, and started to achieve your aims, you will have gained a deeper understanding of how best to put your talents into practice. You will better appreciate where both your strengths and your weaknesses lie, how you relate to the people around you, and how to produce the results you want to see.

On a broader scale, you will have a clearer picture of the position you occupy in the giving ecosystem – and a firmer idea of the position you might want to occupy in the future. As you continue to inhabit and interact with that ecosystem, you will learn and grow. The experience will further nurture you as an entrepreneur and as a human being, encouraging you to discover new and different resources to take with you on your giving pilgrimage. You will gain assurance and dignity and a stronger sense of your place in the world. Tenacity, persistence, consistency and patience will produce rewards. To repeat the words St Paul wrote to the Galatians, 'And let us not grow weary of doing good, for in due season we will reap, if we do not give up.' Through giving, you will get something back.

Another way you will get something back is by becoming a member of the 'tribe' of people who are committed to devoting their talents to changing the world for the better. The word 'tribe', as a manifestation of 'ties', takes its place among the Ts of entrepreneurial giving. You can choose to see this tribe in a philosophical sense as a dispersed mass of people who share an ideology or a set of values and principles. Equally, you can gather the tribe around you in a flesh-and-blood way by doing some research and networking – finding out who's doing what in the world of entrepreneurial giving and then connecting and sharing ideas, experiences and learning.

As you get to know each other, you might well end up helping each other to unearth some more talents and kickstart some new giving projects. By becoming an active member of the tribe, you will find ways of taking yourself further on your personal pilgrimage through entrepreneurial giving.

Your personal progress will also advance the greater cause of entrepreneurial giving as a movement and as a way of being. You will find yourself working still more powerfully for the common good. As you come together as entrepreneurs, taking an innovative, possibly even 'disruptive' approach as you tackle today's challenges, you are looking towards tomorrow. Entrepreneurs are people who tend to lead the way. Where you go, others will follow. You will play a part in building a more generous society.

Since giving is all about you, you are the only person who can map out the route for your giving pilgrimage. Your strategy and your plan of action, growing from your beliefs and values and the talents you have unearthed, will stand as a reflection and expression of your philosophy of life and your ambitions.

As I continue on my giving pilgrimage, I realize how much it continues to teach me about the world and about myself. As an entrepreneur you seize opportunities, make decisions, and face challenges and sometimes criticism. You overcome failures and enjoy successes. Entrepreneurial giving involves so much observation, listening and giving and receiving of feedback. There are always new contacts to be made and networks to be built, results to monitor and assess, and next steps to be considered. Interaction, collaboration and chemistry have such an important part to play.

But just as important for me is the time I take on my own to reflect, meditate and pray, to process all the experiences, probe my responses and recognize where I could have done things differently. Once I've done that, I take some more time to adjust my thinking. Finally, I emerge with a fresh mind and fresh ideas. Sometimes, I even find I've identified another talent to activate in the cause of the common good.

In putting thought, time and effort into this book, I feel I have taken myself further on my giving pilgrimage. I hope it will contribute to the common good by providing entrepreneurially minded people with ideas, examples, encouragement and stimulus as they set out on – or continue – a giving pilgrimage of their own.

As you shape your thinking and your practice, you can move your plans – and yourself – forward by engaging in the art of listening: there is no better way to benefit from other people's knowledge and experiences or to establish the basis of a trusting, fruitful relationship. Further down the line you will build networks and find yourself a place in at least one tribe.

But when it comes down to it, as an entrepreneur in the world of giving you have to rely on yourself. You, and you alone are the source of your inspiration and motivation.

No one else in the world has exactly the same beliefs and portfolio of talent as you. You are the only person on earth who can determine exactly how you choose to use your time. On your pilgrimage you are the one who has to set the pace and the agenda.

In unearthing and activating your talent for giving, your long-term aim is to make the world a better place. As an entrepreneur, you will open yourself to new possibilities, and, through gaining experience and knowledge from each of your ventures, to a sustained process of evolution.

Still more than that, you are taking the opportunity to make yourself a better person. In a generous spirit and with shared benefits in mind, the destination you have set yourself on your giving pilgrimage is the common good. At the same time you are embarking on a journey of self-discovery that promises intellectual enlightenment and emotional fulfilment.

All in all, you stand to gain on every front. What could be better for your spirit and your soul?

ACKNOWLEDGEMENTS

My thanks go to ...

Yehuda Shapiro, longtime Genesis Foundation advisor, collaborator, editor and author, who has transcribed and interpreted dozens of hours of my words, and who, throughout the writing process, challenged me thoughtfully and with great curiosity.

Harriet Capaldi, Genesis Foundation Director of 25 years, who provided constant professional structure and management resources in the planning and production of *A Talent for Giving*.

Nigel Newton, Bloomsbury Publishing's Founder and Chief Executive, for prompting and encouraging me to transform an editorial feature on entrepreneurial philanthropy into a much bigger, more substantial set of ideas, insights and messages.

Robert Willis (1947–2024), poet, cleric and former Dean of Canterbury Cathedral, who advised on the scriptural references in the book and wrote the text for *Angels Unawares*, a new choral work commissioned by the Genesis Foundation from composer Sir James MacMillan.

Evelyna Lamptey-Okine, a spiritually-minded friend and prayer colleague who read a complete draft of the book and provided insights, comments and further direction on the scriptural references and their interpretation.

Chris Levine, longstanding Genesis artist and collaborator, whose pioneering work with light and lasers has gained him international recognition. He was the natural choice to design the cover of this book.

Gail Rebuck, Baroness Rebuck DBE, longtime friend, former Royal College of Art Provost and Penguin Random House publisher and Chair, who recommended *A Talent for Giving* as the title for this book.

Charles Handy (1932–2024), who continually inspired me to consider philanthropy as a way of life.

Joseph McKeen, the inaugural President of Bowdoin College, in Brunswick, Maine, where I studied as an undergraduate. As he declared in 1802: 'Literary institutions are founded and endowed for the common good ... [Every] man who has been aided by a public institution to acquire an education and to qualify himself for usefulness, is under peculiar obligation to exert his talents for the public good.'

John Studzinski

INDEX

AI (artificial intelligence) 79,
　　164–5
AIDS hospices, New York 158
algorithms, social media 79,
　　117
Almeida Theatre 108
anger to compassion and action,
　　transformation of 130–4,
　　163–4
Arise Foundation 146–7, 180
arts and music projects 55–9,
　　86, 105–9, 123–4,
　　135–6, 143–4, 172–3, 180

'being present' 94–6
belonging, sense of 148
Benjamin Franklin House
　　museum 70, 180
the Bible *see* individual books by
　　name
Book of Ecclesiastes 47, 99,
　　121–2
Book of Hebrews 126, 143
Book of Joshua 178
Book of Proverbs 116,
　　117
Business Action on Homelessness
　　134–5

Catholicism 5, 51, 125–6
charity/charitable organizations
　　14, 84–5, 102–3, 109–10,
　　119–20
　　assessment of 110–11
　　membership based 148
children, guidance for
　　98–9
Christophers, Harry 57,
　　107
collaboration and
　　partnerships 47, 68,
　　86–7, 142–51, 172–3,
　　182–4
　　see also networks
comparisons, drawing
　　unhelpful 37
compassion and passion
　　triggers 23–4, 23–4,
　　51–2, 131–4, 163–4
Confession, Catholic 125–6
confidence 78, 80
Covid-19 global pandemic
　　58–9, 108–9
creative projects
　　see Genesis Foundation
criminal networks 146–7
Crowdfunding 162

Darwinism 61
Daughters of Charity 55, 150
Declaration of Independence,
    USA 57, 69
Depaul UK 55
Diana, Princess of Wales 46
dignity, human disabilities,
    support for people
    with 149–50
'disruptors' 63, 130, 183
Donne, John 74
donor and beneficiary
    relationships 77, 83–4,
    85, 149, 171

'echo chambers' 117
educational projects 70, 108
entrepreneurial approach to
    giving 23–5, 59–60,
    180–1
  activated talent 60–1, 133–4
  digital technology *vs* the human
    touch 163–5
  focusing on trigger issues
    131
  identifying opportunities
    through volunteering
    84–5, 169–70
  importance of networks and
    collaboration 71, 86–7,
    139–51, 182–4
  improving existing
    organizations 50–1
  instinct and intuition 62
  introspection and self-
    awareness 177–8

knowing when to leave a
    project 96–7
plans and planning 64,
    170–1
setting realistic goals/project
    size 132, 170–1
the Ts of
  Talent (*see* main entry for
    Talent)
  Technology 47, 144–5,
    162–5
  Temerity. Tenacity.
    Toughness 46, 53, 62–4,
    129, 134–8, 182
  Temperament 45, 131–4
  Tenderness 45–6, 130–1
  Ties. Teams. Tribes 47,
    139–51, 182–3
  Time 44, 89–100
  Transmission 48, 145
  Treasure 44–5, 101–11
  Trials 48, 167–73
  Trust 45, 77–87
  Two 47, 113–27
Epistle of James 133

Facebook 72
failures, learning from 36, 48,
    49, 60, 93, 137, 167–8,
    172
fake news 79
favours, asking for 46
feedback 25, 171
Founding Fathers 67–8
Francis, Pope 8, 146–7
Franklin, Benjamin 67–71, 74–5

Genesis Foundation 55–9, 86,
    105–6, 180
  early endeavours 172–3
  importance of networks
    143–6
  Kickstart Fund 58, 109
  mentoring 123–4
  online Genesis Network
    144–6
  partner organizations 108–9,
    123–4
  Prize 124
  The Sixteen 57, 107, 123
  support during Covid-19
    58–9, 108–9
'gig economy' 143
giving 1, 4, 15–16
  money 3–4, 44–5, 101–11,
    162
  and receiving 153–9
  time 44, 89–100
  see also entrepreneurial
    approach to giving
God 17–19, 28–9, 30, 51, 89, 93,
    158, 178
Gospel of Luke 38, 40
Gospel of Mark 40
Gospel of Matthew 6, 27–30, 40,
    47, 95
gratitude, receiving and 153–9

Hamilton, Alexander
    68
Hamilton musical (L. Miranda)
    68
help, accepting 154–5

helpline project, Operation
    Venus 53–4, 155–6,
    180
heritage projects 70, 180
homeless people, supporting
    54–5, 81, 83–4, 85–6,
    92–3, 125, 134–5,
    150–1, 156–7, 169–70,
    180
human dignity 51, 52–3, 132,
    146–7, 148, 157, 179
human trafficking 146–7, 180
Hume, Archbishop of
    Westminster, Cardinal
    Basil 46, 54–6, 124–6,
    158–9
Hume, David 69
humility 8–9, 154, 171

ideas, sharing 48
instinct/intuition, trusting 62
Internet 161–4
  see also social media;
    technology, digital
Islam 74

Jesus Christ 6, 27–30, 40, 47,
    52, 157
Jewish Literary Foundation
    123
John Paul II, Pope 153–4,
    158–9
journey, giving as a 7
joyfully, giving 1
Judaism 74
Junto 68–9

Knight of St Gregory
 award   158–9

LAMDA   108
libraries   69
Library Company of
 Philadelphia   69
'life hacks'   119
'lightbulb' moments   22
limitations, acknowledging
 your   23, 80
limits, pushing   53
listening, art of   80–3, 118
living in the present   94–6
long-term resources, building
 13–14, 119–20

membership organizations   148
mentors and mentees   24, 47,
 57–8, 61, 87, 114–27
Miranda, Lin-Manuel   68
mistakes, learning from   48, 49,
 60, 93, 137, 167–8, 172
money, giving   3–4, 44–5,
 101–11, 162
'moral science'   70–1
motivation and temperament   45

National Theatre   108, 123
networks   57–8, 68, 87, 122–3,
 139–51, 182–4
 online   144–6

one-to-one meetings   92–3,
 113–27
online networks   144–6
Operation Venus   155–6, 180

Panufnik, Roxanna   55
Parable of the Mustard Seed,
 Gospel of Matthew   40
Parable of the Talents, Gospel of
 Matthew   6, 27–41, 79,
 101–2, 104, 175–6
The Passage project   54–5, 81,
 125, 180
 author's hands-on volunteer
 work   81, 83–4, 85–6,
 92–3, 150–1, 169–70
'passive virtues'   20
peer-to-peer mentoring   118
personal/group identity vs the
 common good   71–5
philanthropy   13–14, 119–20
Philippians, Saint Paul's letter
 to   36
pilgrimages, religious   7–8
pilot projects   170–2
plans and planning   64, 170–1
portfolio of talents   17, 20, 32,
 33, 185
'Power of Two'   47, 113–27
prejudices   72
Psalm   139 19

receiving gifts   153–9
religious sisters   55, 146–7
Riding for the Disabled
 Association   149–50
risk taking   46
role models, contacting   24, 121

Saint Luke's Gospel   157
Saint Matthew   6, 27–41, 79,
 101–2, 104, 175–6

Saint Paul 5, 12, 17–18, 21, 37,
        142–3, 157
    Epistle to the Galatians
        137–8, 182
    letter to the Corinthians 5
    letter to the Ephesians 130
    letter to the Philippians 36
    letter to the Romans 141
Saint Teresa of Ávila 52
Saint Vincent de Paul 55,
        150
schedules, creating and
        keeping 92, 94
self-acceptance 11–12
self-awareness 61, 177–8k
self-belief 61
self-confidence 78, 80
self-trust 78–9
sharing 13
Sixteen, Genesis 57, 107
size/scope of project 132,
        170
slavery 146–7
'sleepwalking' donors 109–10
social media 72–4, 79, 81, 117,
        133, 163
'stars'/celebrities 19
status quo, challenging the 50,
        63
Suzman, Janet 56

talanton 29
talent xi–xii, 2, 4–5, 6, 17–19,
        43, 44, 113–14
    activated 60–1, 133–4,
        185
    asking others' about your 23

    contacting role models 24
    growing/developing your
        35–41
    improving existing
        organizations 50
    'lightbulb moments' 22
    Psalm 139 18
    recognizing/unearthing
        your 18–22, 177–8,
        185
    talent-spotting 142
    trading/bartering 50
    see also Parable of the
        Talents, Gospel of
        Matthew
teams 142–4, 182–3
    see also networks and
        partnerships
technology, digital 47, 72–4, 95,
        144–5, 162–5
    see also social media
temerity 53, 62–3, 102, 120,
        136, 163
temperament and
        motivation 45, 131,
        163–4
tenacity 63–4, 121, 137–8,
        163
tenderness, giving with 45–6,
        130–1
Teresa of Calcutta, Mother 9, 46,
        132, 158, 170
ties see networks
time, giving 44, 89–100,
        114
toughness 129, 134–6
transmission of ideas 48, 145

treasure, money transformed
      to   44–5, 101–11,
      113–14
trials and tests   167–73
triggers, compassion and
      passion   23–4, 51–2,
      131–4, 163–4
trust, importance of   45, 77–87,
      102, 113–14
Two, Power of   47, 113–27

United States Junior Chamber -
      Jaycees   54

volunteering   83–6, 110, 169–70
      see also time, giving

weaknesses, recognizing your
      23
Westminster Cathedral   55–6
Westminster Mass (R.
      Panufnik)   56

X (formerly Twitter)   72

Young Vic Theatre   58, 108,
      144–5